MODERN
FILM
SCRIPTS

P9-DFB-219

IF....

a film by

Lindsay Anderson
and David Sherwin

Simon and Schuster, New York

Published by Simon and Schuster
Rockefeller Center, 630 Fifth Avenue,
New York, New York 10020
First printing

General Editor: Sandra Wake

Frontispiece. Top photograph: Lindsay Anderson and David Sherwin
during the shooting of *If*. . . . Bottom photograph: Lindsay Anderson,
Miroslav Ondricek, Jirina Tvarochova, and Chris Menges during the
shooting of *If*. . . .

SBN 671-20451-3
Library of Congress Catalog Card Number: 70-92182

Manufactured in Great Britain by Villiers Publications Ltd,
London NW5

CONTENTS

ACKNOWLEDGEMENTS

We would like to thank David Sherwin, who gave every assistance in preparing this edition.

Our thanks are also due to Paramount Pictures Corporation for providing stills and loaning us a copy of the film.

Our deepest thanks and gratitude to Lindsay Anderson, without whose assistance this book would never have appeared in its present form.

NOTES FOR A PREFACE

Although both David Sherwin and I went to (different) English Public Schools, *If*. . . . is not to be taken as an autobiographical film, at least not in a narrow or a literal sense. Of course, there are autobiographical elements in the script. For my part, I well remember Fryer, the tall, distinguished College prefect of Cheltondale in winter term 1936, standing at the door before house prayers and shouting at Hughes Hallett beside me: ' Hallett damn you, stop talking!' And the Reverend So-and-So certainly had those nasty habits of smacking you suddenly on the back of the head, and twisting your nipples, if you were unfortunate enough to land in his Maths set.

But such facile tags as ' the Private Hell of the Public Schools ' (*Sunday Graphic*) or ' Hatchet job on the Public School system ' (*Sight & Sound*), are misleading. Essentially the Public School milieu of the film provides material for a metaphor. Even the coincidence of its making and release with the world-wide phenomenon of student revolt was fortuitous. The basic tensions, between hierarchy and anarchy, independence and tradition, liberty and law, are always with us. That is why we scrupulously avoided contemporary references (on a journalistic level) which would date the picture; and why it is completely unimportant whether its slang, its manners, or its details of organisation are true to the schools of this year or that. And this is why the film has been understood — recognised — by so many people, of so many ages, and so many countries.

*

We specially saw *Zéro de Conduite* again, before writing started, to give us courage. And we constantly thought of Brecht, and his definition of the ' epic ' style. David referred to Kleist from time to time. John Ford (' old father, old artificer ') and Humphrey Jennings (romantic-ironic conservative) were in the bloodstream.

9

I have been asked very often about the use of colour in the film — or rather the use of monochrome. When Shelagh Delaney and I were working on the script of *The White Bus,* which was also a poetic film, moving freely between naturalism and fantasy, I remember suggesting that it would be nice to have shots here and there, or short sequences, in colour (it was otherwise a black and white film). The idea also appealed to Miroslav Ondricek, and we did it. Almost no one has seen *The White Bus,* but I like the film very much, and I think the idea was successful.

It was this precedent that gave me the assurance — when Mirek said that with our budget (for lamps) and our schedule he could not guarantee consistency of colour for the chapel scenes in *If. . . .* — to say, ' Well, let's shoot them in black and white.' In other words it was not (of course) just a matter of saving time and/or money. The problem of the script seemed to be to arrive at a poetic conclusion, from a naturalistic start. (Like any fairy-story or folk-tale). We felt that variation in the visual surface of the film would help create the necessary atmosphere of poetic license, while preserving a ' straight ', quite classic shooting style, without tricks or finger-pointing.

I also think that, in a film dedicated to ' understanding ', the jog to consciousness provided by such colour change may well work a kind of healthy *Verfremdungseffect,* an incitement to *thought,* which was part of our aim.

And finally : Why not? Doesn't colour become more expressive, more remarked if drawn attention to in this way? The important thing to realise is that there is no symbolism involved in the choice of sequences filmed in black and white, nothing expressionist or schematic. Only such factors as intuition, pattern and convenience.

This script, as printed here, represents the definitive version of *If. . . .* Unfortunately there is no guarantee that readers will have seen or will be able to see exactly the film we made. It depends where you live. Various versions, differing in various ways from the original, are now circulating through the world. The cuts and modifications demanded by national censorships would indeed provide an interesting footnote to a social history of 1969. In Britain the Board of Film Censors broke precedent by permitting the glimpse of Mrs. Kemp's pubic hair as she wanders naked down the dormitory corridor; but as compensation they demanded the substitution at the start of the shower scene, of an alternative take in which the discreet use of towels prevented an equivalently frank look at the boys. Needless to say the film was forbidden to anyone under the age of sixteen.

The American Board of Censors also gave the film an ' X ' certificate, but passed it unmutilated. The distributors, however, were not prepared to accept the X-rating outside New York, and cut the picture (again Mrs. Kemp and the showers) for an ' A ' rating. Having read about this by chance in *Variety,* we insisted that alternative takes (the same shower scene and a shot of Mrs. Kemp from the rear) be substituted.

Plainly, in this third quarter of the twentieth century since Christ, the naked figure is still the object of deepest alarm. Plainly, also, social reaction, puritanism and philistinism are closely linked. Australia cut the film even for its premiere performance at the Sydney festival and Italy refused to allow it to close the festival at Taormina. (The Italian ban was later rescinded as a result of vigorous protests by the Press.)

Eire was alarmed over various sexual references in the scene in Johnny's study; and South African citizens are not allowed to watch Wallace licking his pin-up, or to hear Mick dreaming of walking naked into the sea with her, making love once, and then dying.

The only instance of purely political censorship so far reported (apart from Portugal, where the film cannot be shown at all) seems to be from the Colonels' Athens, where, as far as we can make out, the film has been showing with its final sequence completely excised.

*

Many people contribute to the making of a film. Many of them get mentioned on no list of credits. For *If. . . .* I would like to record my thanks to Seth Holt who first introduced me to David Sherwin, John Howlett and *Crusaders*; to our patrons, Albert Finney of Memorial and Charles Bluhdorn of Paramount; to Marvin Birdt who stuck his neck out and recommended the script; to my friend Daphne Hunter who suggested the title; people like Peter King and Gerry Lewis, and Mort Hoch who committed themselves to the picture and helped us to get it on the screen; and, of course, David Ashcroft, Headmaster of Cheltenham College, whose liberal understanding and generous help in the creation of a work of art give the lie to facile criticisms of the system of education he believes in. *Floruit, Floret, Floreat!*

I remember also, most gratefully, Pat Moore, for his efficient and effective explosions; Peter Brayham for his fight choreography; Sergeant Instructor Rushforth for his beautiful performance on the bar, and Michael White and Malcolm Miles who helped us out so well on their motor-bikes on the Cheltenham-Tewkesbury road.

*

Essentially the heroes of *If. . . .* are, without knowing it, old-fashioned boys. They are not anti-heroes, or drop-outs, or Marxist-Leninists or Maoists or readers of Marcuse. Their revolt is inevitable, not because of what they *think,* but because of what they *are.* Mick plays a little at being an intellectual ('Violence and revolution are the only pure acts', etc.), but when he acts it is instinctively, because of his outraged dignity, his frustrated passion, his vital energy, his sense of fair play if you like. If his story can be said to be 'about' anything, it is about freedom.

In this sense Mick and Johnny and Wallace, and Bobby Phillips and the Girl are traditionalists. It is they, not their conformist elders nor their conformist contemporaries who speak the tongue that Shakespeare spoke ('We must be free or die'). 'England Awake,' Johnny cries in the gym. And Mick: 'We are not cotton-spinners all: Some love England and her honour yet!' and Wallace, as he lunges, 'Death to tyrants!' They are very, I suppose fatally, romantic. Theirs is still: 'The homely beauty of the good old cause.'

Far indeed from filling me with dread, I find the last sequence of the film exhilarating, funny (its violence is so plainly metaphorical), a bit shocking, magnificent (when the Headmaster is shot between the eyes), and finally sad. It doesn't look to me as though Mick can win. The world rallies as it always will, and brings its overwhelming fire-power to bear on the man who says ' No.'

> *Charge once more then, and be dumb;*
> *Let the victors when they come,*
> *When the Forts of Folly fall,*
> *Find thy body by the wall!*

LINDSAY ANDERSON
November 1969

CREDITS:

Screenplay by	David Sherwin
from the original script	
Crusaders by	David Sherwin & John Howlett
Directed by	Lindsay Anderson
Produced by	Michael Medwin and
	Lindsay Anderson
Production company	Memorial Enterprises Ltd.
Music composed and	
conducted by	Mark Wilkinson
Sanctus from the	Les Troubadours du Roi
'Missa Luba'	Baudouin (Philips recording)
Assistant director	John Stoneman
Assistants to the director	Stephen Frears and Stuart Baird
Director of photography	Miroslav Ondricek
Cameraman	Chris Menges
Sound recordist	Christian Wangler
Dubbing editor	Alan Bell
Dubbing mixer	Doug Turner
Camera operator	Brian Harris
Camera assistant	Michael Seresin
Assistant to the producers	Neville Thompson
Casting director	Miriam Brickman
Production manager	Gavrik Losey
Production accountant	Brian Brockwell
Production designed by	Jocelyn Herbert
Editor	David Gladwell
Assistants to the editor	Ian Rakoff and Michael Ellis
Interpreter	Jirina Tvarochova
Production secretary	Zelda Barron
Wardrobe	Shura Cohen
Make-up	Betty Blattner
Continuity	Valerie Booth
Construction manager	Jack Carter
Electrical supervisor	Roy Larner
Transport	Jim Hughes
Electrical contractors	Lee Electrics
Production processing	Humphries Laboratories

14

Length	10,005 feet
Running time	111 minutes
Made on location in	England
and at	Coefficient Film Facilities Ltd., London
Distributed in Great Britain and the United States of America by	Paramount Pictures Corporation

CAST:

Crusaders

Mick	Malcolm McDowell
Johnny	David Wood
Wallace	Richard Warwick
The girl	Christine Noonan
Bobby Phillips	Rupert Webster

Whips

Rowntree	Robert Swann
Denson	Hugh Thomas
Fortinbras	Michael Cadman
Barnes	Peter Sproule

Staff

Headmaster	Peter Jeffrey
General Denson	Anthony Nicholls
Mr. Kemp	Arthur Lowe
Matron	Mona Washbourne
Mrs. Kemp	Mary Macleod
Chaplain	Geoffrey Chater
John Thomas	Ben Aris
History master	Graham Crowden
Classic master	Charles Lloyd Pack
Music master	John Garrie

School porter	Tommy Godrey

Seniors

Stephans	Guy Ross
Keating	Robin Askwith
Pussy Graves	Richard Everitt
Peanuts	Philip Bagenal
Cox	Nicholas Page
Fisher	Robert Yetzes
Willens	David Griffin
Van Eyssen	Graham Sharman
Baird	Richard Tombleson

Juniors

Machin	Richard Davies
Biles	Brian Pettifer
Brunning	Michael Newport
Markland	Charles Surridge
Jute	Sean Bury
Hunter	Martin Beaumont
Salesman	Ellis Dale

IF . . . .

Shot 1.
Fade in on Paramount's trademark.
Shot 2.
Fade to a black background, Boys' *voices singing the College song, off.*
Boys' *voices singing off, to the tune of '* Stand up, stand up, for Jesus ' : ' Stand up ! Stand up ! For College,
        Each manly voice upraise . . .'
The following title card fades in, accompanied by organ music, and the Boys' *voices singing.*

Title :   ' *Wisdom is the principal thing;*
            therefore get wisdom:
            and with all thy getting
            get understanding.'
                       Proverbs IV: 7

Fade out and then fade in.
*Shot 3. (Black and white stock, sepia tint.)
The main credits come up over a print of the College in near silhouette, sepia tint, seen from the playing fields, as the boys continue to sing, off. (Still on page 2) The *main title lettering is scarlet, the other credits are white.*
Boys' *voices, off* : ' Clasp each the hand in brotherhood,
        And raise the roof with praise.'
The credits continue to fade in and out.
Boys' *voices, off* : ' And when these days of school are past,
        Though near we be or far,
        We'll stand again for College,
        Who made us what we are.'
The credits continue to fade in and out, but the music stops and the sound changes to banging and crashing and running footsteps. Boys *can be heard shouting and chattering. Then a wild, uncontrollable giggling. Then music begins again (now orchestral) and the credits finish. The print of the College fades out.*

17

1

Shot 4. TITLE :   COLLEGE HOUSE
                   . . . Return

Fade out.

Shot 5.

Fade in to a corridor of the school, crowded with BOYS *coming and going, pushing and shoving each other, shouting news, shrieking. They are all wearing black suits with stiff collars; Juniors in short jackets, Seniors in tail-coats. Ties black, with a red, white and blue stripe — the College colours.*

Shot 6.

High angle medium close-up of a BOY *dragging his trunk. A small* BOY *jumps on to it and rides along. Camera pans with them as they pass.*

Shot 7.

In low angle medium shot, more BOYS *carry trunks, trays, hockey sticks, etc. up and down the narrow stairs. The general shouting, banging and chattering continues.*

Shot 8.

Camera cuts to another low angle medium shot of the stairs. Two small BOYS *labour under an enormous trunk.*

Shot 9.

Medium shot of MARKLAND *who bursts out of a doorway on the left, carrying his loaded trunk tray. He collides with* MACHIN. *Both boys are about fourteen. There is a clatter as a tin of baked beans falls to the floor.*

MARKLAND *furious* : Machin, you bloody shag !

Camera pans right and tilts down as MACHIN *plays hockey with the tin and runs out of shot.*

Shot 10.

Seen from above in medium shot, more BOYS *carrying trunks up the stairs towards camera, and trays downstairs to their studies.*

Shot 11.

In the background, ROWNTREE *makes his way down-*

stairs through the mêlée. ROWNTREE *is a tall young man, wearing the distinctive silk embroidered waistcoat of the* WHIPS, *the prefects of the school. Camera pans with him as he reaches the bottom of the stairs and turns towards camera. (Still on page 2)*

ROWNTREE : Run in the corridor!

Shot 12.

Medium long shot, from above, of BOYS *in the corridor; two of them carrying chairs on their heads.*

ROWNTREE *off* : Run!

The BOYS *start to run along the corridor. Camera pans with them.*

Shot 13.

Cut to more BOYS *seen in high angle medium long shot, jostling in front of a notice-board at the end of the passage. More* BOYS *pass in the foreground. There is less noise and many of the* BOYS *are taking notes from the notice-board.* JUTE, *a very small boy, stands bewildered at the edge of the crowd.*

Shot 14.

A high angle medium shot of the group, with STEPHANS *and* BILES *in the foreground.* JUTE *pushes forwards through the crowd. He turns to* STEPHANS *who is older and taller than most of the others.*

JUTE : Excuse me, I can't see my name. I'm new.

STEPHANS *without turning* : You don't speak to us. You're scum, aren't you?

JUTE *bewildered* : I don't know.

Several BOYS *turn to stare. Their faces contrast with* JUTE'S *childish one.*

BILES : 'Course he's a scum.

MARKLAND *pushes* JUTE *roughly back into the crowd.*

MARKLAND : You're blocking my view, scum.

ROWNTREE *yelling the scum-call, off* : SC-UU-UUU-MMM!

Shot 15.

Camera cuts to another high angle shot of the group round the notice-board. Before ROWNTREE *has finished his screaming bellow, all the younger* BOYS *run away down the corridor into long shot, leaving* STEPHANS *and*

JUTE *standing.* JUTE *realises he ought to go too and runs off after them. The sound of running footsteps echoes through the corridor.*
Shot 16.
Long shot of SCUM *running towards camera. Camera tracks back to reveal* ROWNTREE *in medium shot, standing next to a pile of luggage and some golf clubs. In medium shot,* SCUM *shuffle to a halt in front of* ROWNTREE.
ROWNTREE *imperiously* : Biles, Markland.
BILES *and* MARKLAND *stand alert.*
ROWNTREE : Biles, take these to my study, and this, and watch those eggs.
He loads BILES *with a set of golf clubs — and a box of groceries. The rest of the* SCUM *begin to drift off.*
Shot 17.
Low angle medium close-up of ROWNTREE. BILES *staggers past with his gear. (Still on page 3)*
ROWNTREE : Markland, warm a lavatory seat for me. I'll be ready in three minutes.
Shot 18.
In high angle medium close-up, JUTE *stands puzzled as* MARKLAND *trots off.*
Shot 19.
Low angle medium close-up of ROWNTREE, *looking down.*
ROWNTREE : And who are you?
Shot 20.
Reverse angle shot of JUTE, *looking up.*
JUTE : Please, Sir, I'm Jute.
Shot 21.
Back to ROWNTREE *looking down at him.*
ROWNTREE *amused* : Are you indeed? *He calls after one of the* BOYS. Brunning!
Shot 22.
Cut to a long shot of the corridor, past medium close-up of JUTE. MARKLAND *is seen running off.* BRUNNING *turns away from the notice-board and runs up to* ROWNTREE *and* JUTE.

Shot 23.

Back to ROWNTREE *in low angle medium close-up.*
ROWNTREE *looking down* : This is Jute. You're Jute's Bumph
Tutor. Take him to the Sweat Room.

Shot 24.

High angle medium long shot of JUTE *and* BRUNNING, *as
they walk away from* ROWNTREE, *who stands back to
camera.*
ROWNTREE : And Jute. *They pause and look back at him.*
You don't call me Sir. *They walk on* . . . Run!

Shot 25.

Low angle medium close-up of ROWNTREE.
ROWNTREE : *Run* in the corridor!

Shot 26.

*The Sweat Room: the Junior boys' study and common
room. Medium shot as* BOYS *mill about. There is a
general buzz of chatter and the occasional shout or bang
of books on desks. Two* BOYS *are fighting and shouting
on the floor.* BRUNNING *and* JUTE *appear in long shot
at the door at the end of the room.* BRUNNING *walks in
towards camera.* JUTE *stands watching two wrestling*
BOYS *who are blocking his path. (Still on page 3)*

Shot 27.

High angle medium close-up of BRUNNING *as he walks
along the line of partitions, to find a spare place for* JUTE.
One BOY *sits with his feet up on the desk, picking his
nose.*

Shot 28.

Cut back to a high angle medium close-up of JUTE
*nervously watching the progress of the fight. Close-up of
the* BOYS *as they pass, wrestling.*
BRUNNING *off* : Jute!

Shot 29.

Medium long shot of BRUNNING, *by the desks. Other*
BOYS *are crossing in and out.*
BRUNNING : Hey, Jute!

Shot 30.

Medium shot as JUTE *makes his way forward, past the
line of cubicles.* BOYS *sit or stand about, sorting out*

*their things and talking. Camera tracks back and pans
with him as he passes, until he reaches* BRUNNING. *Hold
in medium shot on both.*

BRUNNING *indicating a cubicle* : This is your place. Books and
magazines here . . . *he shows him* . . . food in the locker . . .
points . . . pin-ups over here. *He indicates the back wall.*
Okay?

Shot 31.

MACHIN *is seen in medium long shot, back to camera,
pinning a notice on the board. He moves back towards
a large desk, and taps it loudly.*

MACHIN : Silence in the Sweat Room !

Shot 32.

Medium long shot of the Sweat Room as the BOYS *look
in* MACHIN'S *direction. The chatter and noise dies down.*

MACHIN *off* : I would like to remind the Sweat Room that no
tinned or potted foods are allowed . . .

Shot 33.

Cut back to a medium shot of MACHIN.

MACHIN : . . . except tinned fruit and baked beans without
meat. *One* BOY *comes forward and stands near the desk,
back to camera. There are general groans of protest, off.* Shut
up !

Shot 34.

Low angle medium long shot of BOYS *watching* MACHIN.

MACHIN : Duty scumming list now up. Junior table and
exercise lists up in five minutes.

Shot 35.

Shot of MACHIN.

MACHIN : Get on with it. MACHIN *sits down and the* BOYS
start moving about and talking again.

Shot 36.

Medium shot, from above, of MARKLAND, *carefully
unwrapping some large peaches at his desk. He sniffs
one and places it on the shelf under his desk.*

Shot 37.

Low angle medium shot of the staircase. BOYS *are carrying empty trunks away to store in the loft. Camera pans
left and tilts down as* PHILLIPS *walks down. His way is*

barred by GRAVES *and* KEATING. *He pushes past them: they lean over the stair-rail.*

KEATING *taunting* : Come on up, Bobby.

GRAVES : We want to stroke you.

DENSON *off* : You two !

DENSON, *another* WHIP, *comes into medium shot. He gestures to the* BOYS.

DENSON : Get upstairs and behave yourselves. *To* PHILLIPS.
And you, Phillips, stop tarting.

KEATING *and* GRAVES *carry on upstairs.* PHILLIPS *also starts to move on.*

PHILLIPS : I'm not tarting.

DENSON *brushes* PHILLIPS' *hair up with his cane* : You need a hair-cut.

PHILLIPS *disappears hurriedly along the corridor.* MICK *comes into shot, balancing his suitcase on his shoulder. He is wearing a large black overcoat, a black, broad-brimmed hat and a very long black scarf wrapped round the lower half of his face. Camera tilts up as he looks at* DENSON *as they pass, and goes on upstairs. Footsteps and shuffling can be heard.*

STEPHANS *off* : Right . . .

Shot 38.

Cut to the Senior Dormitory. It is early evening by now. In a high angle medium long shot, STEPHANS *can be seen standing between the rows of beds and partitions. Other Senior boys are unpacking trunks on their beds. Camera pans with* STEPHANS, *walking across the room.*

STEPHANS *continuing* : . . . get a move on, you've got thirty minutes to get out and get your trunks up into the loft.

Shot 39.

Medium shot of MICK *coming into the dormitory, still carrying his case and wearing hat and scarf. He looks round briefly. Camera pans and stops with him. (Still on page 4)*

STEPHANS *off* : Oh God !

Shot 40.

Camera cuts to a high angle medium shot of STEPHANS, *with* JOHNNY, WALLACE *and others in soft focus behind*

27

him. They are all seen from Mick's *point of view and are all looking at him.*

Stephans : It's Guy Fawkes back again.

Shot 41.

High angle shot of Mick; *he acknowledges no one and walks forward. He passes* Peanuts, *a thin, bespectacled* Boy *who is sitting on his bed fiddling with bits of a telescope.*

Peanuts : Hello, Michael.

Johnny *off* : Hello, Mick.

Camera tracks back and pans with Mick, *as he goes to the last vacant bed. Track in until he reaches the bed and throws his case on to it.* Stephans *comes into shot, passes* Mick, *camera panning with him, till* Wallace *is included in the shot. He makes a face as* Stephans *speaks.*

Stephans : You've got twenty-nine minutes left.

Wallace : Oh, can it, bog-face.

He moves away. Johnny *is behind him.*

Johnny : Lay off it, Stephans, you're monotonous already.

Stephans : Being lippy, Knightly? *He tosses a pile of* Johnny's *things into the air.* Tidy this disgusting mess. *A bright light flashes in his eyes and he turns sharply.*

Shot 42.

Medium close-up of Peanuts, *focusing the setting sun into* Stephans' *eyes with the mirror of his telescope.*

Shot 43.

Medium close-up of Stephans *squinting into the light.*

Stephans : What the hell's that?

He goes out of frame.

Shot 44.

High angle medium shot of Peanuts *holding the telescope.* Stephans *walks into frame. He stops by* Peanuts *and picks up the telescope, turning to the others.*

Stephans : Hey! Peanuts has come back with a bloody ray gun. *(Still on page 4)*

Shot 45.

Low angle medium shot of Wallace *and* Johnny *looking across the dormitory.*

28

STEPHANS *off* : It's a bloody ray gun.

WALLACE : God, Stephans, you're so ignorant. Anyone can see it's a shag-spot burner.

JOHNNY : Clear your face up in a couple of seconds.

PEANUTS *off* : Actually . . .

> *Shot 46.*
>
> *Cut back to* PEANUTS *and* STEPHANS *in high angle medium long shot, as* PEANUTS *retrieves the telescope.* STEPHANS *looks embarrassed. He has very bad acne.*

PEANUTS *continuing* : . . . it's a six-inch standard reflecting telescope.

STEPHANS *annoyed* : Well, get it out of here. *He walks back towards camera* . . . Knightly . . .

> *Shot 47.*
>
> *Close-up of* MICK, *looking up, eyes peering out from under his hat and over his scarf.*

STEPHANS *continues, off* : . . . stop preening yourself in that mirror. MICK *looks towards* JOHNNY. Preen, preen . . .

> *Shot 48.*
>
> *Medium long shot of* JOHNNY *looking at himself in a hand-mirror.* WALLACE *stands on his right, by the next bed.*

STEPHANS *off* : . . . preen and pride.

> JOHNNY *throws the mirror down on the bed. Thump.*
>
> *Shot 49.*
>
> *Medium shot of* STEPHANS, *sneering;* PEANUTS *busy with his telescope in the background.*
>
> *Shot 50.*
>
> *Medium shot of* JOHNNY *as he picks a magazine out of his trunk tray and looks towards camera.* WALLACE *is reading in the foreground. Camera pans with* JOHNNY *as he goes over to* MICK *and hands him the magazine.* MICK *glances at it, nods, sits down on a bed, and begins to flick through it.* JOHNNY *goes out of shot and* MICK *continues to look at the magazine.* STEPHANS *comes across to him.*

STEPHANS : Travis, you're in the House — take that crap off.

> MICK *takes no notice, so* STEPHANS *tries to pull his scarf off.* MICK *pulls away quickly, holding the scarf*

*close to his face, camera panning with him. He picks up
his trunk tray. A* Boy *jumps him from behind, trying
to pinion his arms.* Mick *shakes himself violently free
and scoots down the dormitory and out through the
door. General shouting.*
Shot 51.
High angle shot of the stairs. Denson *is coming up as*
Mick *rushes down, carrying his trunk tray.* Mick
barges past.

Denson : Travis!

Mick *turns, without stopping.*

Mick *innocently* : Sorry, Denson.

Shot 52.
Mick's *study: a tiny, poky room, a few oddments on the
shelves, fragments of last term's pin-ups on the walls.
Medium shot as* Mick *eases his way through the door
with his tray. Camera pans and tilts down as he carries
it through and puts it down. Music begins over. He
walks back, camera panning and tilting with him, and
stops, looking towards a small mirror on the wall.*
Shot 53.
Medium close-up of Mick's *reflection in his mirror as
he walks towards it. He takes off his hat, and slowly
unwinds the scarf from his face. He reveals a moustache.
As he sighs, the music stops and he reaches for a pair
of scissors and starts to cut his moustache. The silence is
broken by thumping, off.*
Shot 54.
Camera tilts up to Johnny, *seen in medium close-up
climbing through the top of the partition. A post-card
of a grinning Mao is propped against the wall.*

Johnny *grinning* : God, you're ugly. You look evil.

Mick *off* : Yeah . . .

Shot 55.
Medium close-up of Mick *still snipping at his moustache,
his face reflected in the mirror.*

Mick : My face is a never-failing source of wonder to me.

Shot 56.
Medium shot, from below, of Johnny *as he climbs down.*

30

Camera tilts down and pans with him as he comes over to the window.

JOHNNY : What did you grow it for? *He sits down.*

MICK *throwing his coat down* : To hide my sins.

JOHNNY *looks at the contents of* MICK'S *trunk tray: an old leather fighter-pilot's helmet; a string of human teeth; a relief map of the world; a poster-size reproduction of a Bert Stern photograph of Marilyn Monroe; motor-cycle scramble shots from a magazine; records, books, scotch-tape, tins, a large spoon, motor-cycle goggles, toy handcuffs. He picks up the string of teeth.*
Shot 57.
Low angle medium close-up of MICK *shaking a canister of shaving cream and squirting it on his face.*

VOICE *off* : SCU-UU-MMM!
Shot 58.
Back to JOHNNY *in medium shot. The sound of running footsteps can be heard somewhere outside the room.*
Shot 59.
Low angle medium close-up of MICK, *back to camera, shaving with a cut-throat razor.*

JOHNNY *off* : What do you think of him?
Shot 60.
High angle medium shot of JOHNNY *holding a picture of an American Negro soldier, lurching forward with a sub-machine gun, in a magazine.*
Shot 61.
Low angle medium close-up of MICK, *with half his moustache shaved off, looking at the picture. (Still on page 21)*

MICK : Fantastic!
Shot 62.
Shot of JOHNNY *holding the picture. (Still on page 21)*

MICK *off* : Put him right in the middle.
Shot 63.
Back to MICK, *shaving and looking at* JOHNNY *off, whom we hear tearing the picture out of the magazine.*
Shot 64.
Medium shot of JOHNNY *who gets up and scotch-tapes*

31

the picture to the wall, camera tilting up and panning with him. Music begins over.
Shot 65.
Medium shot of MICK, *stepping forward to look at it. Camera pans until* JOHNNY *comes into shot.*
MICK : Fan-tas-tic!
Shot 66.
Close-up of the picture. The figure is violent, massive. The music stops.
Shot 67.
Medium close-up of MICK, *as he goes back to his shaving again.*
JOHNNY *off* : Do you know what I did this summer? Built a hut in the woods. Lived there for three weeks . . .
MICK *turns towards him.*
Shot 68.
Medium shot of JOHNNY.
JOHNNY : . . . by myself, 'till I ran out of food . . .
Shot 69.
Medium close-up of MICK *shaving again. He chuckles.*
Shot 70.
JOHNNY *in medium shot again* : It was an experiment in asceticism. Penetrating the inner core of my being. You do anything good?
Shot 71.
MICK, *in close-up, shaving, back to camera.*
MICK : I met this fantastic bird in the East End, went round all the pubs.
Shot 72.
Medium shot of JOHNNY *unrolling the poster.*
MICK *off* : You ever been to those pubs? You should see those . . .
Shot 73.
Cut back to close-up of MICK *wiping his face with a towel.*
MICK : . . . old loves dancing, showing their knickers. Take 'em off near the end.
Shot 74.
Medium shot of JOHNNY. *They both laugh.*

Shot 75.

Slightly low angle medium close-up of Mick. *He turns and takes a bottle of 'After Shave' off the shelf.*

Mick : She had a weird religion. Only kiss on Thursdays. *He pats lotion on to his face and neck.* Took me home to meet her Mum and Dad. Well, that finished it. Practically married us off, they did, over the Sunday joint.

A bell clangs loudly and insistently, off. Mick *grimaces at the noise.*

Shot 76.

Cut to medium close-up of Johnny, *depressed.*

Shot 77.

Low angle close-up of Mick *turning in* Johnny's *direction.*

Mick : When do we live, that's what I want to know?

General hubbub, off . . . the bell stops ringing.

Shot 78.

High angle long shot of the Dining Hall. About sixty Boys *are coming in to take their places, milling around and shouting generally, in between the refectory tables. They line up at their appropriate tables. Seniors, Middles, Juniors.*

Shot 79.

Medium shot of one of the Senior tables, where Mick *and* Johnny *already have places, opposite* Stephans, *who is standing back to camera.*

Mick *indicating the place opposite* : Wally !

Johnny : Hey, Wallace ! Woolly-Bum, come with us !

Shot 80.

Wallace *looks across, and moves past other* Boys *till he reaches* Stephans, *whom he elbows out of the way. He grins across at* Mick *and* Johnny *now opposite him.* Stephans *sulks.*

Shot 81.

Cut to another table. Medium shot of Cox *and* Pussy Graves.

Pussy : Come on, we're gonna have our tiny parts inspected. *He starts to pull out his shirt.* Cox *looks down.*

Cox : 'E's not wearing a *vest* already, is 'e ?

Shot 82.

Medium shot of KEATING *and* FISHER *at the end of the table.*

KEATING : Pass the message down to Biles : ' Biles, why are you a freak ? '

Camera pans along the line as FISHER *passes the message.*

FISHER : ' Biles, why are you a freak ? '

Track continues as JACKSON *passes the message to* BILES.

JACKSON *quietly* : ' Biles, why are you a freak ? '

BILES *not looking at him* : Shag off, you creeps !

JACKSON *smirks. (Still on page 22)*

Shot 83.

Medium long shot from above, as FORTINBRAS, *another* WHIP, *stalks with conscious dignity into the Dining Hall. The* BOYS *turn towards him and the noise dies down.*

Shot 84.

High angle medium shot of BRUNNING *and* JUTE *standing at the Junior table.*

BOY : Sssh !

BRUNNING *lecturing* JUTE : Now listen. You've got to know all the seniors' names. Ask me who someone is.

Shot 85.

Cut to high angle medium shot of FORTINBRAS *looking in their direction.*

FORTINBRAS : Brunning, damn you, stop talking !

Shot 86.

Shot of BRUNNING *and* JUTE. BRUNNING *sticks his tongue in his cheek. He does not seem to care.*

Shot 87.

High angle medium long shot of FORTINBRAS. *He walks back to the door. There is a moment's pause—then footsteps off.* MR. KEMP, *the Housemaster,* MATRON *in white coat and large white wimple,* MRS. KEMP, ROWNTREE, JOHN THOMAS, *the Under-master are joined by* FORTINBRAS, *who is followed by* DENSON *and* BARNES *as they all march into the room in single file.*

Shot 88.

High angle medium long shot as they process through

34

the Dining Hall. Camera pans with them until they end up in a line behind the top table.

MR. KEMP *clearing his throat* : This term, I've just one thing to say to you . . . one rule. Follow it and you won't go wrong. And it is this : work—play—but don't mix the two.

Shot 89.

Reverse angle of the Dining Hall, the Junior table in the centre. All the BOYS *are looking towards the top table.*

MR. KEMP *off* : Perhaps some of you new boys are a little bewildered by the rapid succession of events which has overtaken you since your arrival, but you'll soon find your way about.

Shot 90.

Cut to a medium shot from below of MR. KEMP *at the table,* ROWNTREE *beside him,* MR. THOMAS *and* MRS. KEMP *behind.*

MR. KEMP : Just remember that life here is a matter of give and take.

Shot 91.

Medium shot of MRS. KEMP, *a faded, middle-aged woman, who looks perpetually vague.* MATRON *beside her, a little forward, scanning the* BOYS' *faces. Businesslike, but (she thinks) kindly.*

MR. KEMP *off* : We are your new family, and you must expect the rough . . .

Shot 92.

Low angle medium shot of BARNES, FORTINBRAS, *and* DENSON. FORTINBRAS *caresses his lips with the silver knob of his cane. (Still on page 22)*

MR. KEMP *off* : . . . and tumble that goes with any family life; we're all here to help each other.

Shot 93.

Cut back to a low angle medium shot of MR. KEMP, ROWNTREE *by his side, the others behind. (Still on page 23)*

MR. KEMP : You will find here in College House, a discipline not only to help others, but also to help yourselves.

Shot 94.

Medium shot of the Middle School table, PUSSY GRAVES

35

looking straight ahead.

Mr. Kemp *off :* Help the House and you will be helped by the House.

Shot 95.

Medium shot of Mr. Kemp. *There is a short pause and he looks uncomfortable. Someone coughs. He collects himself and motions* Mr. Thomas *to come forward.*

Mr. Kemp : Now I'd like to extend a warm welcome to our new Under-master, Mr. Thomas. I'm sure you'll all help him to find his feet.

Mr. Thomas *smiles awkwardly and shuffles back to his place as* Rowntree *steps forward, making sure that* Mr. Thomas *has no time to speak; camera pans with him to a medium shot of* Rowntree *with* Denson *standing at his shoulder.*

Rowntree : Last summer, this House got itself a reputation for being disgustingly slack.

Shot 96.

Medium shot of Mick, Johnny *and* Wallace *looking bored, and* Stephans *looking attentive.*

Rowntree *off :* This term, things are going to be different. If there's any repetition of that deplorable lack of spirit . . .

Shot 97.

Low angle medium shot of Rowntree *with* Denson, Mr. Thomas *and* Mr. Kemp *behind.*

Rowntree *continuing :* . . . I shall come crashing down on offenders.

Shot 98.

High angle shot of Pussy Graves *and* Cox. Cox *purses his lips and looks down. He hates this.*

Rowntree *off :* We don't intend to carry passengers. *Pause.* I'd like to remind the House that it's Winter Term . . .

Shot 99.

High angle long shot of the top table, across the Boys.

Rowntree : . . . and that lock-up is at five p.m. Anyone leaving the House after that time must have a leave signed by a Whip. The town, of course, is out of bounds. Line up in the usual way for medical inspection.

Mr. Kemp *leaves the room hurriedly.* Denson *bangs the*

bell on the table.

DENSON : Line up here!

FORTINBRAS : Alphabetical order!

The BOYS *begin to file out from the tables towards the top table. There is general chattering.*

BARNES : Stop talking!

FORTINBRAS : Quiet!

Shot 100.

Medium shot of DENSON *and* FORTINBRAS *who sit down with lists in front of them.* DENSON *rings the bell again with a flourish. The* BOYS *start to shuffle forward,* BILES *first. He stands in front of* DENSON.

FORTINBRAS *to another* BOY, *out of shot* : Health certificate?

DENSON *at the same time* : Ringworm?

BILES : No.

FORTINBRAS : Ringworm?

DENSON : Eye disease?

BILES : No.

FORTINBRAS : Eye disease?

DENSON : V.D.?

BILES : No.

FORTINBRAS : V.D.?

DENSON : Confirmation class?

BILES : No.

FORTINBRAS : Confirmation class?

DENSON *waves* BILES *on. The next* BOYS *move forward.*

DENSON : Next! BILES *moves out of shot, followed by* COX.

FORTINBRAS, *rustling his papers* : Next!

PEANUTS *stands in front of* DENSON. *The interrogation continues, more or less without pause.*

DENSON : Confirmation class. Ringworm?

PEANUTS : No.

FORTINBRAS : Ringworm?

DENSON : Eye disease?

PEANUTS : No.

FORTINBRAS : Eye disease?

DENSON : V.D.?

PEANUTS : No.

DENSON : Confirmation class?

PEANUTS : *No.* DENSON *waves* PEANUTS *on.*

FORTINBRAS : Confirmation class?

DENSON *to the next* BOY : Wake up, you!

> *Pan along the table as more* BOYS *file up. Pan continues to show* ROWNTREE *and* MR. THOMAS *sitting in the background, watching the proceedings.* ROWNTREE *is chatting graciously to* MR. THOMAS.

FORTINBRAS *off* : Next!

DENSON *off* : Certificate.

> *Shot 101.*
>
> *Medium shot of* MATRON *and* BARNES *standing at the end of the table.* BILES *stands in front of them, back to camera.*

DENSON *off* : Ringworm?

> MATRON *signals* BILES *to lower his trousers.* BILES *does so revealing spindly white legs. Camera tilts down as* MATRON *peers down and inspects him with a large torch. (Still on page 23)* BARNES *lifts* BILES' *shirt tails with his cane. On the sound track, the examination continues, off.*
>
> *Shot 102.*
>
> *The Senior Dormitory. It is bedtime. High angle medium long shot of* BOYS *in a line washing in small tin bowls which rest on a bench down the middle of the room.* MICK *stands at the end, his towel round his neck. He sings, conducting with his toothbrush.*

MICK *and* OTHERS *singing* :

> Stand up! Stand up! For Jesus,
> The buggers at the back can't see.

STEPHANS : Quiet in the washroom!

> *The singing continues as a mumble.*

STEPHANS *shouting* : Quiet!

KEATING : Look at Fatso's blubber!

> *Shot 103.*
>
> *Medium shot as* FISHER, *the fat boy, pulls off his shirt. It sticks round his head exposing a large expanse of fat midriff.* KEATING *has grabbed the folds of flesh round* FISHER'S *stomach and he swings him round, exhibiting him.*

38

KEATING: It's disgusting! It's a disease! FISHER *grapples with him, enfolding him. They totter together to a bed.* Christ, I'm infected, I've got elephantiasis!

Other BOYS *come into shot and they all grapple with* FISHER, *who disappears under a pile of* BOYS.

Shot 104.

Medium long shot of WALLACE *drying himself with a scarlet towel. He looks up at the noise, and jumps onto his bed. Camera tracks with him as he vaults over the partition and dives onto the struggling* BOYS. STEPHANS *comes in and starts to drag them off* FISHER.

STEPHANS *shouting*: Get out of it! Get out! Come on, move it! Go on, Keating, get out. *Pause. Everyone moves away.* STEPHANS *walks away, sneering.* Fatso hasn't got elephantiasis —he's just a fat Jew.

MICK *comes over and leans against the partition, his sponge in his hand.* STEPHANS *walks past him.*

MICK: Watch it, Spotty.

Pan with STEPHANS *walking down the dormitory.* JOHNNY *is seen in medium shot, sitting in his bed.*

JOHNNY: You're not a Whip yet.

STEPHANS *turns.*

STEPHANS: Look, any more lip from you two, you'll be down for a cold shower.

MICK'S *sponge hits him full in the face,* STEPHANS *swings round, furious.*

Shot 105.

Cut to the dormitory corridor. Long shot of DENSON *and* BARNES *walking towards camera. A* BOY, *in dressing gown and slippers, shuffles from behind the camera, and disappears through a dormitory door.*

DENSON *and* BARNES *shouting*: Dormitory inspection in three minutes!

*Shot 106. (Black and white stock, sepia tint.)

The narrow staircase leading up to MR. THOMAS'S *room.* MRS. KEMP *is coming up the stairs, followed by* MR. THOMAS, *in high angle medium shot.*

MRS. KEMP: The central heating doesn't come this far, I'm afraid. *She disappears round a corner of the staircase.*

39

Mrs. Kemp *off* : But the room itself is quite warm.

Pan with Mr. Thomas *as he follows her up on to the landing. Medium shot of them as* Mrs. Kemp *unlocks the door of a room right at the top. The Chapel clock chimes in the distance. She opens the door and switches on the light. The room is small, dingy and sparsely furnished.*

Mrs. Kemp : It's a little bare, but . . .

*Shot 107.

Medium long shot as Mrs. Kemp *comes into the room, followed by* Mr. Thomas.

Mrs. Kemp : . . . Mr. Britton made it very snug. *She closes the small dormer window.* The marvellous thing is you're completely quiet up here. You can see the chapel spire when the leaves fall. Mr. Thomas *puts down his suitcase and looks around.* Have you a shilling? *She moves over to a small gas fire.*

Mr. Thomas : Oh, yes. *He gives her one.*

She puts it into the obviously empty meter. It falls with a metallic clatter.

Mrs. Kemp : Do come down and see us if you're at all lonely.

Mr. Thomas : Thank you so much, Mrs. . . . Kemp.

She goes out, closing the door on him as he speaks. He walks over to the bed and sits down disconsolately.

Voice *off* : Junior Dormitory inspection now !

Shot 108. (Return to colour.)

Cut to the Junior Dormitory. High angle medium shot of Jute *sitting in bed writing in a large notebook. He hears the door open and looks up.*

Shot 109.

Medium shot of Barnes *standing at the dormitory door. Camera pans from right to left as he walks towards the* Boys, *sitting in bed.* Jute *is the only one engaged in any kind of activity, all the rest are just sitting in bed.* Barnes *walks down the line of beds, looking closely at all of them, camera tracking with him. Pan as he draws level with* Jute's *bed. He takes the book out of* Jute's *hands.*

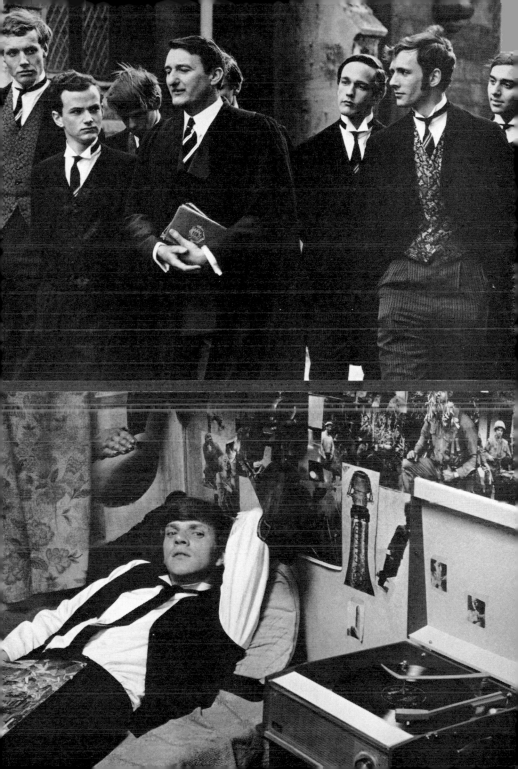

BARNES : What's this?

JUTE *looking up nervously* : My diary.

BARNES : Well, keep it downstairs in the Sweat Room. *He hands it back.*

> *Camera tracks and pans across as* BARNES *walks into medium close-up.*

BARNES : All right, good standard, Machin. Keep it up. Good night.

BOYS *together* : Good night.

> BARNES *goes out.*
> *Shot 110.*
> *Cut to the Senior Dormitory. Low angle medium close-up of* MICK, *gargling.*

STEPHANS *off* : Come on, Travis, stop showing off.

> MICK *looks sideways, then spits into a bowl. Pan with him as he walks back to his bed, combs his hair and takes off his dressing gown, hanging it carefully on the hook behind the bed.*

VOICE *off* : Senior Dormitory inspection now.

> MICK *leaps neatly into bed, and freezes. The camera tilts down with him.*
> *Shot 111.*
> *Medium long shot as* ROWNTREE, FORTINBRAS, *and* DENSON *come into the room, and stop by* PEANUTS' *bed.*

ROWNTREE : Good evening.

> *Shot 112.*
> *Medium shot of* STEPHANS *sitting up neatly in bed.*

STEPHANS *nodding in the* WHIPS' *direction* : Good evening.

> *Shot 113.*
> *Pan with the three* WHIPS *as they walk round the dormitory.* ROWNTREE *and* FORTINBRAS *are in the lead.* DENSON *walks over to* MICK *and flicks his hair with his cane.*

DENSON : Your hair's too long. Get it cut !

> *He turns on his heel and walks out of frame.* MICK *laconically raises two fingers after him.*
> *Shot 114.*
> *Long shot of* DENSON, *now with* ROWNTREE *and*

45

FORTINBRAS *at the end of the room.*

ROWNTREE : Otherwise very good, Stephans. Lights out in thirty seconds. Good night.

They turn to leave. There is a murmur of voices.
DENSON *peers over the partition.*

DENSON : No talking ! Silence.

Shot 115.
Medium shot of MICK *in bed. He begins a slow hand-clap.*

MICK : Jolly, jolly good, Stephans.

Shot 116.
Medium shot of STEPHANS *sitting smugly in bed. Clapping is heard off.*
Shot 117.
Medium shot of JOHNNY *leaning up in bed, also clapping.*

JOHNNY : Jolly, jolly good, Stephans. Jolly, jolly good.

Camera pans across to WALLACE, *sitting in the next bed.*

WALLACE *joining in* : Jolly, jolly good, Stephans. Jolly, jolly good.

Pan continues past the partition to reveal STEPHANS *in bed.*

STEPHANS : You three had better watch it.

JOHNNY *off* : Don't push us . . .

Shot 118.

JOHNNY *in high angle medium close-up* : . . . Stephans, the day is coming.

Shot 119.
Medium shot of WALLACE *and* STEPHANS *on either side of the partition.*

STEPHANS : What day?

WALLACE : One night we're going to massacre you, Stephans. I'll do you for free.

DENSON *bellowing, off* : Townside windows and skylights open tonight.

*Shot 120. (Black and white stock, sepia tint.)
Cut to a low angle shot of the outside of the House, with all of the windows blazing with light.

VOICE *off* : Lights out ! *All the lights go out simultaneously,*

except one. A dog barks somewhere in the distance.
  *Shot 121. (Black and white stock, magenta tint.)
  Cut back to the Senior Dormitory, now in darkness. The
  wash bowls gleam.
MICK : Stephans, whatever you're doing now—don't.
STEPHANS : Quiet.
WALLACE : Peanuts, Peanuts is it true you've become a Buddhist?
PEANUTS : What?
JACKSON : Christ, don't you know Buddhists believe in being immoral? They worship sex. *A pause.*
PEANUTS : You mean Hindus. Hindus worship sex . . .
STEPHANS : Shut up. Go to sleep.
PEANUTS : Paradise is for the blessed—not for the sex obsessed.
  Fade out.[1]

---

[1] End of reel one.

2

Shot 122. Title :   COLLEGE
             ' *Once again assembled . . .*'
Fade out.
Shot 123.
*A general shot of the College, seen across the playing
fields. The massed voices of the whole College can be
heard singing a hymn.*
School *singing, off* : ' Who would true valour see,
                      Let . . .'
Shot 124.
*Cut to a low angle long shot of one of the chapel
windows from the inside.*
School *singing, off* : '. . . him come hither . . .'
*Shot 125. (Black and white stock, magenta tint.)
*High angle long shot of the whole school gathered ın
the Chapel, singing. Each house is assembled in blocks of
pews facing inwards.*
School *singing* : ' Here's one will valiant be,
                      Come wind . . .'
*Shot 126.
Close-up of Jute *looking desperately through his hymn
book for the right page. He looks towards the hymn book
of the* Boy *next to him.* Brunning, *who is behind* Jute,
leans forward and whispers the number to him. Jute
begins to sing.
School *singing* : '. . . come weather.
                      There's no discouragement . . .'
*Shot 127.
High angle medium long shot of some Boys *standing,
including* Stephans.
School *singing* : ' Shall make him once relent . . .'
*Shot 128.
Medium shot of Mr. Thomas *and* Mr. Stewart *in
the* Masters' *seat behind the* Boys. Mr. Stewart *looks
round wearily as he sings.*

SCHOOL *singing*: ' His first avowed intent
            To be a pilgrim.'
*Shot 129.
High angle long shot of the rows of BOYS *with the*
MASTERS *in the highest row of pews behind them, all*
singing.
SCHOOL *singing*: ' Since Lord, Thou dost defend . . .'
*Shot 130.
Medium close-up of MR. KEMP *mouthing the words.*
He looks round nervously.
SCHOOL *singing, off*: ' Us with Thy spirit . . .'
*Shot 131.
Medium shot of the BOYS, *standing in line, singing.*
*Shot 132.
Low angle medium shot of the ladies in the gallery:
MRS. KEMP, MATRON *and the* MASTERS' *wives, all*
singing.
SCHOOL *singing, off*: ' Shall life inherit.'
*Shot 133.
Low angle medium shot of the HEADMASTER, *singing*
lustily, and other MASTERS *and* BOYS *in foreground.*
SCHOOL *singing*: ' Then fancies flee away!
            I'll fear not what men say . . .'
*Shot 134.
Medium shot of the CHAPLAIN *standing behind the choir*
boys.
SCHOOL *singing*: ' I'll labour night and day,
            To be a pilgrim.'
*Shot 135.
The hymn finishes. High angle long shot of the whole
Chapel. There is a pause, interspersed with coughs and
the scuffling of feet.
CHAPLAIN *off*: Let us pray.
Everyone kneels down.
Shot 136. (Return to colour.)
Outside the Chapel. Music begins: an organ voluntary,
high and staccato. The side door opens, and BOYS *begin*
to stream out, scooping up piles of books from the
ground.

49

Shot 137.

Very long shot of the Chapel and College buildings. BOYS *stream out of the cloisters and begin to spread out through the College.*

Shot 138.

Medium shot of the HEADMASTER *and the* MUSIC MASTER *as they come out of the main door of the Chapel together and walk towards camera. Other members of the Staff follow behind. The* HEADMASTER *calls to someone out of shot. He is the super-executive, effortlessly in control.*

HEADMASTER: Ah, Rowntree. *To* FINCHLEY, *the College porter, who hands him a book to be signed.* That'll be all thank you, Finchley. ROWNTREE *comes up to the* HEADMASTER. I want to see all Whips in my study after break.

ROWNTREE: Right, Sir. *He turns to go.*

HEADMASTER: Oh, how was India? Enjoy it? Jolly good. *A young master,* MR. BRIDGES, *is passing.* Bridges, Bridges. I shall be taking the modern sixth for business management this term. I hope you don't mind. ROWNTREE *goes.*

MR. BRIDGES: Yes, yes, of course, Headmaster.

> MR. KEMP *bustles up and stops at the* HEADMASTER'S *elbow.*

MR. KEMP: Headmaster . . .

HEADMASTER: One moment, Kemp. *To* BRIDGES: I've made it late school, Thursday. Is that okay? *To* KEMP: Yes, Kemp, sorry.

> *Camera tracks slightly with them as they walk along the path.*

MR. KEMP: Headmaster, may the dramatic society use your study for their Monday readings?

> *The* HEADMASTER *stops, camera holds with him.*

HEADMASTER: Oh well, I'll have to come back to you on that one, Kemp. MR. KEMP *hurries off, disgruntled, as the* CHAPLAIN *comes up to join the* HEADMASTER. Padre, that was a super voluntary you gave us this morning. What was it—eighteenth century?

CHAPLAIN: Buxtehude, Headmaster.

HEADMASTER: Really? Well, it was lovely. *They part.*

50

Shot 139.

Medium long shot down the cloisters. The BOYS *are making their way down to the classes, the Junior* BOYS *running and shouting in medium shot.*

Shot 140.

Cut to MR. STEWART'S *classroom. Medium shot of some of the Senior* BOYS *coming into the room, walking towards camera.* KEATING *is throwing out books from a table on the dais beneath the blackboard.*

GRAVES : Here, you've heard what's happened to the orchestra this term? No girls from Springfield—complete ban.

General moans. DENSON *moves out of shot towards a desk. The others are finding desks and sitting down.*

KEATING : Why?

GRAVES : Oh, their breasts were getting too big—temptations of the devil . . .

STEPHANS *is sitting on a desk in the middle, picking his spots and inspecting the results on his finger.*

COX : How will we survive?

MICK *walks across to* STEPHANS.

MICK : Excuse me, do you mind not picking your shag-spots in here? *General laughter.*

Shot 141.

Reverse long shot of the classroom. STEPHANS, *annoyed and embarrassed, gets up, turns, and sits down at his desk.*

STEPHANS *stiffly* : I think it best if we ignore each other this term.

JOHNNY *comes over and sits down next to* MICK *in the front row.*

JOHNNY : How the hell can we, with you spewing pus all over the room?

More laughter.

DENSON *sitting behind* MICK : You drips.

JOHNNY *turning round* : Shut up!

MICK *blows a raspberry at the same time.*

DENSON : Shut up, Travis.

MR. STEWART *singing, off* : ' Then fancies flee away,

I'll fear not . . .'

Shot 142.

Long shot of the corridor outside. MR. STEWART *cycles round the corner, gown flying, riding on past camera, still singing.*

MR. STEWART *singing* : '. . . what men say,
I'll labour night and day . . .'

Shot 143.

Medium shot of MR. STEWART *riding smoothly through the doorway and dismounting.*

MR. STEWART *singing* : '. . . To be a pilgrim ! '

KEATING *takes the bike from him and props it up against the wall.* COX *closes the door, and the camera pans, following* MR. STEWART *as he strides across in front of the desks, still humming* : ' Ta-ta-tum tum-ta-ta-ta-tum . . .' *He goes over to the window and opens it wide, taking a few deep breaths. He then turns to face the class, the lion-tamer back in the cage. Pan with him as he takes some papers out of a canvas bag slung over his shoulder and tosses them vaguely in the direction of the* BOYS *he is addressing.*

MR. STEWART : Your holiday essays. Graves, charming. Keating, good—making an effort at last. Denson, bad. Cox—Stephans, distribute. *He passes the rest of the papers over.*

Shot 144.

High angle medium shot of COX *handing them round.* MR. STEWART *walks nonchalantly back to his desk, out of shot.*

MR. STEWART *off* : I'm afraid, Michael Travis, I lost your essay somewhere in the Mont Blanc tunnel . . . but I'm sure it was good.

Camera pans past COX *to reveal* JOHNNY *and* MICK *who pass essays back.* MR. STEWART *bangs and thumps books down on the desk, off.*

MR. STEWART *off* : Right !

Shot 145.

Medium shot from above as MR. STEWART *throws himself into his chair. He tilts it right back, stretches his arms behind his head, fists clenched, and begins.*

MR. STEWART : Ah . . . Europe in the nineteenth century

and the growth of nationalism . . . *Pause—then he continues very rapidly.* In studying the nineteenth century, one thing will be clear—that the growth of technology, telegraph, cheap newspapers, railways, transport—is matched by a failure of imagination, Denson, a fatal inability to understand the meaning and consequences of all these levers and wires and railways. Climaxing in . . .

Shot 146.

Long shot of the Boys *in the classroom, from* Mr. Stewart's *viewpoint.* Mick *and* Johnny *in the front row. Impassive expressions.* Stephans *is quietly picking his spots.* Keating *chews his pen.*

Mr. Stewart *off* : . . . 1914 when the German Kaiser is told by his generals that he cannot stop the war he has started because it would spoil the railway timetables upon which victory depended.

Shot 147.

Medium shot of Mr. Stewart *leaning back on his chair. He stares at the class, then leans forwards over the desk. The chair legs land noisily.*

Mr. Stewart : Or perhaps you fashionably and happily believe it is all a simple matter of evil dictators—rather than whole populations of evil people like . . . ourselves? *He stiffens. A note of desperation.* Do you disagree? Don't you find this view of history facile?

Shot 148.

The Boys, *still impassive A slightly tighter shot than 146. Silence.* Mick *smiles at* Johnny.

Mr. Stewart *off* : No? *Pause.* Do you have a view?

Shot 149.

Another pause. Medium long shot from above of Mr. Stewart *behind his desk, seen over the heads of the* Boys. Mr. Stewart *stands up and walks across to the window, camera panning with him.*

Mr. Stewart : Well, if you insist on staring at me like a lot of Christmas puddings, you can at least write. Perhaps you'll allow me to teach you—Travis—to make drudgery divine. It has been said . . .

He stands by the window and leans against the wall to

pull his trouser-bottoms out of his socks.
Shot 150.
Cut to a medium shot from above of MICK *leafing through his book.*

MR. STEWART *continuing, off* : . . . of George the Third that ' he was a mollusc who never found his rock '.
Shot 151.
Medium shot from below as he addresses the class, his gaze settles on MICK.

MR. STEWART : . . . Said by whom . . . er, Travis?
Shot 152.

MICK *looking up* : Plumb? J. H. Plumb.
Shot 153.
Medium close-up of MR. STEWART, *his eyes glaze a moment.*

MR. STEWART : Possibly . . . *He walks decisively out of shot.*
Shot 154.
Medium shot of JOHNNY, STEPHANS *and others, with* MICK *smiling in medium close-up.*

MR. STEWART *off* : What were the failures . . .
Shot 155.
Low angle medium long shot of MR. STEWART, *the camera pans with him as he walks round towards his desk.*

MR. STEWART : . . . of the British Constitution and the political parties that prevented the mollusc king from finding his rock? A twenty minute essay . . . without notes.
He sits down and tilts back his chair, puts his feet up on the desk, and takes the Daily Express *out of his pocket.*
Shot 156.
Medium close-up of DENSON. *He leans forward as* MICK, *seen from behind, turns to dip his pen in* DENSON'S *ink-well.*

DENSON *whispering* : What's a mollusc for God's sake?
Shot 157.
Medium close-up of MICK, *with* MR. STEWART *in soft focus in the background.* MICK *aims his pen at* DENSON *with a deadly expression, then flicks it contemptuously into his face. He turns away with a jaunty sneer.*

54

Shot 158 .

Cut to a low angle shot of a Gothic window from the outside. Desks can be seen through it.

CHAPLAIN *off* : Two triangles are congruent when one fits exactly over the other.

Shot 159.

Cut to the classroom, from the inside. The CHAPLAIN, *seen from behind, is giving a geometry class to the Juniors. Medium shot of the* CHAPLAIN *walking down between the rows of desks past the window.*

CHAPLAIN : The sides of the one equal the sides of the other. The angles of the one equal the angles of the other. Understand, Brunning?

BRUNNING : Yes, sir.

The CHAPLAIN *smacks* BRUNNING *hard across the back of his head.*

CHAPLAIN : Good ! Sine 'A' equals 'BC' over 'AB' . . . *Pan with him as he walks on, to the desk where* JUTE *is sitting. Camera tilts down as the* CHAPLAIN *suddenly puts his hand inside* JUTE'S *shirt. He grips his nipple and twists it hard. . . .* equals the perpendicular over the hypotenuse. JUTE *squirms with pain.* Right, Jute ?

JUTE *squirming* : Yes, sir. *(Still on page 24)*

Shot 160.

Cut to a medium shot from below of one of the Chapel windows, from the outside.

HEADMASTER *off* : College is a symbol . . .

Shot 161.

Cut to a similar shot of a statue in a niche.

HEADMASTER *off* : . . . of many things. *Footsteps are heard off.*

Shot 162.

Medium shot of the HEADMASTER *with a group of* WHIPS, *including* ROWNTREE, *walking across the Chapel court in a group. Camera tracks with them. (Still on page 41)*

HEADMASTER : Scholarship, integrity in public office, high standards in the television and entertainment worlds . . . *They stop and look out of shot* . . . huge sacrifice in Britain's wars.

VOICE *yelling, off* : Eyes . . .

Shot 163.

Long shot of a platoon of cadets from the College Corps marching across frame, the playing fields behind them. On the command they all look towards the HEADMASTER, *out of shot.*

VOICE *yelling, off* : . . . left !

Shot 164.

Medium shot of the HEADMASTER *and* WHIPS *watching, as the* CADETS *pass by. The* HEADMASTER *acknowledges them gravely, and walks on.*

HEADMASTER : Of course, some of our customs are silly . . . *off* . . . you could say we were middle-class.

Shot 165.

Long shot of a Gothic façade, seen across grass. A GROUNDSMAN *rests immobile, with his roller by the wall. The* HEADMASTER'S *group pass him as if he was not there.*

HEADMASTER : But a large part of the population is in the process of becoming middle-class, and many of the middle class's moral values are values that the country cannot do without. We must not expect to be thanked . . .

Shot 166.

Medium shot of the group. Pan with them as they move towards camera, the HEADMASTER *pausing briefly to emphasise a point.*

HEADMASTER : Education in Britain is a nubile Cinderella, sparsely clad and much interfered with. *The* WHIPS *laugh dutifully, and they move on out of shot.*

Shot 167.

Overhead long shot of the quad, grass in the centre. The group appears through an archway and continues along the path.

HEADMASTER : Britain today is a power house . . . of ideas, experiments, imagination, on everything from pop-music to pig-breeding; from atom power stations to mini-skirts, and that's the challenge we've got to meet.

Shot 168.

Medium long shot, low angle, as they walk across a

56

balcony, camera panning along with them.

HEADMASTER : There are boys in College in whom the muscles of creativeness are flexing, the pinions of imagination twitching. *The group stops again.* That's what makes my job worth doing. That's what makes College an exciting place. *He looks out over the balcony: the pioneering general surrounded by his faithful lieutenants.*

> *Shot 169.*
> *Close-up of a painting of the College Founder : a shrewd Tudor look. Clattering can be heard off.*
> *Shot 170.*
> *High angle long shot of four Junior* BOYS *laying the tables.*
> *Shot 171.*
> *Medium close-up of the portrait of a former headmaster.*

BRUNNING *off* : John Thomas?

JUTE *off* : Tom Thomas.

> *Shot 172.*
> *Medium shot of* JUTE, *sitting in his cubicle in the Sweat Room.* MARKLAND *is sitting opposite him and* BRUNNING *is standing over him, leaning against the partition.*

MARKLAND : The Headmaster?

JUTE : Flossie.

BRUNNING : The Chaplain?

JUTE : Um . . . Chippy Wood.

> *Shot 173.*
> *Low angle medium close-up of* BRUNNING, *tetchy.*

BRUNNING : No, it *isn't* ' Um . . . Chippy Wood '.

> *Shot 174.*
> *Medium close-up of* MARKLAND, *impatient.*

MARKLAND : It's Chippy Wood.

> *Shot 175.*
> *Low angle medium close-up of* BRUNNING.

BRUNNING *crossly* : When Rowntree tests you, you've got to be word . . .

> *Shot 176.*
> *Medium close-up of* MARKLAND.

BRUNNING *off* : . . . perfect. Any umming and erring and you're done for.

57

Shot 177.

BRUNNING *in low angle medium close-up* : Now the town—and no mistakes.

Shot 178.

Medium close-up of JUTE, *from above.*

MARKLAND *off* : Town girls?

JUTE : Town tarts.

BRUNNING *off* : Grammar school?

JUTE : Smudges.

BRUNNING *off* : All others?

JUTE : Bloody oiks.

BRUNNING *emphasising, off* : Oiks.

Shot 179.

Low angle medium close-up of BRUNNING, *as he removes his glasses.*

BRUNNING : Listen. You do realise it's not just a matter of *knowing* the answers. It's how you say it.

Shot 180.

Medium close-up of MARKLAND.

MARKLAND : One word wrong and you'll fail the whole test.

BRUNNING *off* : And *we* get beaten.

MARKLAND : And you have to take the test all over again.

Shot 181.

Low angle medium close-up of BRUNNING, *replacing his glasses.*

BRUNNING : Right . . . Raising boaters?

Shot 182.

Medium close-up from above of JUTE, *looking up.*

JUTE : Boaters must be raised to masters, wives . . .

Shot 183.

Medium close-up of BRUNNING, *from below.*

JUTE *off* : . . . and friends of College.

BRUNNING *darts forward shouting* : No! Masters, *their* wives and *the* friends of College.

JUTE *off* : Masters, their wives and the friends of College.

Shot 184.

BRUNNING *turns towards* MARKLAND *and sighs with exasperation. Medium close-up of* MARKLAND, *looking resigned.*

Shot 185.
Medium close-up from below as BRUNNING *turns to look towards camera.*
Shot 186.
Medium close-up, high angle, of JUTE, *forlornly apologetic.*

JUTE : I'm sorry Brunning.

Shot 187.
Cut to MICK'S *study at night. A collage covers the wall, photographs clipped from newspapers, magazines, Sunday supplements: weapons of war; soldiers in Vietnam; D-Day corpses floating in the sea; the young Lenin in the disguise of his Polish exile; the Pope raising his hands in prayer . . . on the sound track, the ' Sanctus ' chorale from the* Missa Luba *begins, very loud.*

Shot 188.
High angle medium long shot of MICK *lying on the couch: there are magazines beside him, and on the floor a litter of cut-out pictures. He adjusts the tone of the record-player. He leans back (Still on page 41) and then leafs through a copy of* Paris Match *until he finds a picture that he wants to cut out.*

Shot 189. ·
Medium shot of MICK *cutting the picture from the magazine. The ' Sanctus ' goes into a drumming passage and he leans forward to move the needle back to the beginning of the chorale. The ' Sanctus ' begins again. Camera tilts down as he lets the picture fall on to the floor, following it until* MICK *is out of shot. It shows a lion resting, powerful but in watchful repose, in the branches of a tree. It falls among other pictures of wild animals.*

Shot 190.
The House Gym: shouting and yelling. BILES *runs from behind camera, pursued by* KEATING *wildly flailing a belt,* GRAVES *wielding a broom-handle,* BRUNNING *and* WILLENS. *Their footsteps thud on the wooden floor. They chase* BILES *round the vaulting horse, then back, trapping him between the parallel bars.* KEATING *lashes*

at his hands with the belt, and GRAVES *beats a tattoo on the floor with his broom. (Still on page 42)* BILES *runs back into the corner: the others close in on him, scoop him up, and carry him out, screaming and kicking.*
Shot 191.
The lavatories: high angle long shot over the centre line of urinals. Camera pans as KEATING *and* GRAVES *carry* BILES *in and down the line of lavatories.* BRUNNING *and* WILLENS *shriek excitedly.*

KEATING : You love this . . .

GRAVES : You love it !

BILES : You shits.

GRAVES : Let's eat him—get his trousers !

Hold as WALLACE *is revealed sitting on a lavatory seat, strumming a guitar. He frowns at the noise as the others carry* BILES *past.*
Shot 192.
High angle shot of KEATING *and* GRAVES *holding* BILES. *He struggles as* WILLENS *pulls off his trousers. They are all shouting.*

KEATING *hysterically* : I'm eating him, I'm eating him !

Pan left to right and tilt up to the level of the partition tops, as they carry BILES *into a cubicle and heave him upside down, hauling his legs up to the cistern.*

GRAVES : Oh, dirty ! You've been learning dirty habits. Look out, wash him !

KEATING *and* OTHERS : Right ! Wash him ! Wash him !

WALLACE'S *guitar-playing can be heard dimly, off.*
Shot 193.
High angle medium close-up of WALLACE *sitting on the lavatory. The shouting continues off. He pauses in his strumming. (Still on page 42)*

WALLACE : Hey ! Turn it up !

Shot 194.
Medium close-up of BRUNNING *and* WILLENS *tying* BILES' *feet to the cistern with* KEATING'S *belt and a tie. Camera tilts down to a close-up of* GRAVES *and* KEATING *holding on to his bare legs. They are all shouting at the tops of their voices.*

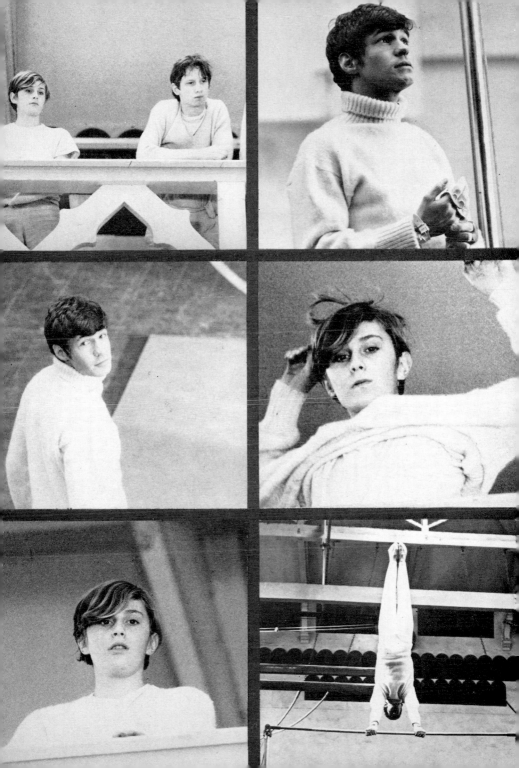

Shot 195.

High angle medium close-up of BILES' *head being lowered into the lavatory bowl.*

KEATING : How do you like that, Biles?

Shot 196.

Medium close-up of GRAVES *and* KEATING *hanging on to the struggling* BILES. *Camera pans right, losing* KEATING. GRAVES *is very excited and keeps shouting :* ' There we are ! '

Shot 197.

Close-up of BILES *being lowered into the bowl again. One of the others pulls the chain, flushing the water round his head.*

Shot 198.

Medium shot of WALLACE *playing his guitar again. He leans forward and peers round the door of his cubicle The screaming and shouting mingles with the sound of the cistern filling.*

KEATING *off* : You love it, Biles, you love it !

WALLACE *shouting* : Shut up !

Shot 199.

Medium close-up of KEATING *and* GRAVES *holding* BILES' *legs.*

KEATING *viciously* : Don't you? Enjoying it?

Shot 200.

Close-up of BILES' *head being lowered into the bowl again. He is roaring. The chain is pulled again to the accompaniment of a rising crescendo of shouting.*

Shot 201.

High angle shot of KEATING *and* GRAVES *holding* BILES' *legs. They decide to call it a day and all jump down towards camera, coming into close-up before going out of shot. Camera tilts up slowly over* BILES' *body and skinny legs to a medium close-up of his feet on either side of the cistern. The* BOYS *can be heard giggling as they hurry out.*

Shot 202.

High angle medium long shot of KEATING, GRAVES, WILLENS *and* BRUNNING, *running out of the lavatories,*

pushing and jostling each other.
Shot 203.
Medium shot of BILES, *hanging motionless from the cistern. (Still on page 42) Camera is tilted at right angles so his whole body is in shot. There is a moment's pause, then the sound of a lavatory flushing.*
Shot 204.
High angle medium long shot of WALLACE *emerging from his cubicle, putting on his coat. Camera tilts as he walks towards it. He looks curiously into* BILES' *cubicle.*

WALLACE *wearily* : For God's sake, Biles.

Pan continues as he walks in. Tilt up as he reaches up to the top of the cubicle and unties BILES' *feet.*
Shot 205.
Medium close-up of WALLACE *as he helps* BILES *down. Camera tilts up to a medium close-up of* BILES *as* WALLACE *moves out of shot.* BILES' *face is very pink and his soaking hair drips down his face. Pan with* BILES *as he moves towards camera.*

BILES : Excuse me, please, you're standing on my clothes.

Shot 206.
The Chapel. About thirty new BOYS *are sitting in the choir stalls on one side of the aisle.* JUTE *is in the front line.*

MUSIC MASTER *off* : Stand up.

The BOYS *all get to their feet.*

MUSIC MASTER *off* : Fortissimo. All together. One, two, three . . .

The harmonium begins to play.

BOYS *singing* : ' Stand up ! Stand up ! For College,
                Each manly voice upraise . . .'

Shot 207.
Medium shot of the CHAPLAIN *seated at the far end of the Chapel.* STEPHANS *is kneeling, head bowed, back to camera. The* BOYS *can be heard singing the hymn off, while the* CHAPLAIN *and* STEPHANS *talk.*

STEPHANS : I keep having them, Sir, these thoughts . . .

CHAPLAIN : What kind of thoughts?

STEPHANS : Dirty thoughts.

CHAPLAIN *guardedly* : We all have temptations to withstand.

STEPHANS : It's too strong for me, Sir.

CHAPLAIN : Fight the good fight, Stephans.

Shot 208.

High angle medium shot of STEPHANS *past the* CHAPLAIN. *He looks at the* CHAPLAIN, *uncomforted. Then he lowers his head. The* CHAPLAIN *lays his hand on* STEPHANS' *hair. The singing stops. Fade out.*

3

Shot 209. TITLE: TERM TIME

Fade out.

Shot 210.

Quick fade in: medium shot of JUTE *running hard and dodging excitedly during a rugger game. Camera tracks back to reveal the game in progress, and then tracks in again and pans with* JUTE. *The players are shouting at each other.*

Shot 211.

Medium long shot of the field. Track with the running, jostling players, the ball at their feet.

MR. THOMAS *in the background, running with them*: Run! Run! Run! Run! Run! Feet! Feet! Feet!

Shot 212.

Medium close-up of BOYS *running with the ball. They go out of shot revealing* JUTE *in medium close-up.*

MR. THOMAS: Go . . . Go on Jute.

Camera tracks with JUTE *as he runs.*

Shot 213.

Long shot of MR. THOMAS *in tweed jacket and long khaki shorts, running with the* BOYS, *shouting and blowing his referee's whistle and gesticulating wildly. They all run into medium long shot, camera tracking with them.*

MR. THOMAS: Run, run, run, run, run, run! Fee-eet!

Shot 214.

Medium close-up of JUTE *and one or two other* BOYS *jigging about, waiting for the ball to come out of a scrum.*

MR. THOMAS *off*: Feet! Get it out! Get it out! Get it out!

Shot 215.

Long shot of MR. THOMAS *running out from the scrum with the ball tucked under his arm, being chased by most of the* BOYS.

MR. THOMAS: Forward pass! Follow! Follow! Follow! Go

low, go low!

Camera pans and tracks with him as he runs. He swerves and comes towards camera. Both teams are chasing him, with about eight BOYS hanging on to his jacket, but he goes on running, dragging them along. Tilt down and hold in high angle medium shot as he is finally brought down and disappears under the BOYS, who are shouting with laughter.

*Shot 216. (Black and white stock, sepia tint.)

Cut to a low angle long shot of the House at night. Linking music.

Shot 217. (Return to colour.)

Cut to a high angle shot of MATRON in the Senior Dormitory, pushing a basket trolley full of clean linen, MACHIN padding beside her. She is distributing clean shirts and collars. MACHIN takes the clothes as she ticks off the names on her list, and puts them on the lockers.

MATRON: Travis . . . Cox . . . Graves . . . Jackson . . . Pearce and Keating. I've told all the boys it's going to be a white Christmas, and I'm always right. It's my seaweed . . . Fisher . . . Page.

She pushes the trolley into the foreground, followed by MACHIN. Music.

Shot 218.

Cut to close-up of the back of PHILLIPS' head. The music stops.

Shot 219.

Long shot of Whips' Common Room. PHILLIPS is toasting muffins over the blazing fire. ROWNTREE sits in an armchair on one side, DENSON on the other, and BARNES sits by a table in medium shot, back to camera. DENSON is watching PHILLIPS surreptitiously. FORTINBRAS leans against a locker on the right, his eyes also on PHILLIPS. Framed groups on the walls; a 19th century painting of some state occasion over the fire, Julie Andrews stuck into a corner of the frame.

Shot 220.

High angle medium shot of PHILLIPS taking the muffin off the toasting fork. Camera pans as he stands up and

69

puts the plate of muffins on the small table beside
Rowntree. *(Still on page 43) The pan continues and
takes in* Denson, *watching* Phillips.
Rowntree *off* : A bit closer. Phillips *moves the plate nearer
to him.* Thank you, Phillips.
　Shot 221.
　Long shot (as 219). Phillips *stands by the table.*
　Rowntree *sits to his left,* Denson *to his right.* Rowntree
　puts down his newspaper.
Rowntree : What are these?
Phillips : Muffins.
Rowntree *picking one up and inspecting it* : I thought I
specifically ordered crumpets.
Phillips : I couldn't get any. I thought these would do.
Rowntree : It's not up to you to think.
Phillips *looking down* : Sorry, Rowntree.
　Shot 222.
　Medium close-up of Barnes *watching: his eyes flick
　between* Phillips *and* Rowntree.
Rowntree *off* : Oh, go away, lazy sod!
　Phillips *walks past* Barnes, *not looking at him.*
　Shot 223.
　Long shot as Phillips *walks towards the door, past*
　Barnes *and* Denson *in the background, and*
　Fortinbras. *Pan with* Phillips *as he goes out and
　then pan with* Fortinbras *as he walks back to the table
　and takes a muffin.*
Fortinbras : He gets a little lovelier each day.
Rowntree : He's a lazy little bugger.
Fortinbras : I'll swap you. Ah, muffins. I *love* muffins.
　Fortinbras *goes over and sits by the large table oppo-
　site* Barnes. Barnes *sits up and leans over to take a
　cake from a plate on the table.*
Barnes : You and your wholesome Bobby Phillips, you're
driving us all mad with . . .
　Shot 224.
　High angle medium shot of Denson. *He looks annoyed
　and puts his cup down on the table beside him.*
Barnes *off* : . . . jealousy.

70

FORTINBRAS *off* : Do you know what Partridge in Haigh House said to me?

Shot 225.

Medium long shot of FORTINBRAS *and* BARNES.

FORTINBRAS : He said, ' Why don't you send Bobby Phillips on a scum call to us one night . . .'

Shot 226.

Medium close-up of ROWNTREE *buttering a muffin.*

FORTINBRAS *off* : '. . . and we'll send you our Taylor '.

ROWNTREE *interested* : Which one's Taylor?

Shot 227.

Medium long shot of FORTINBRAS *and* BARNES.

BARNES : You know, that little blond. Mmm. *He blows a kiss.*

Shot 228.

Medium shot of DENSON *sitting in his armchair.*

DENSON : Oh, don't be disgusting.

Shot 229.

Medium shot of ROWNTREE, *eating a muffin.*

ROWNTREE : What's the matter, Denson, aren't you keen?

BARNES *off* : Denson's not like the rest of us—he's got standards.

Shot 230.

Medium long shot of FORTINBRAS *and* BARNES, *laughing.*

FORTINBRAS · Purity Denson.

Shot 231.

Medium shot of DENSON.

DENSON : It's just a matter of setting an example. If *we* can't set an example, who can? That's why we're given our privileges.

Shot 232.

Medium shot of ROWNTREE.

ROWNTREE : Admirable sentiments.

Shot 233.

Medium shot of DENSON *retiring behind a newspaper.*

DENSON : Anyway, this homosexual flirtatiousness is so adolescent.

Shot 234.

Medium long shot of FORTINBRAS *and* BARNES. *They exchange amused glances.*

Shot 235.
Medium shot of ROWNTREE. *He puts down his muffin,*
eyeing DENSON *speculatively.*
ROWNTREE : Let's just see. *He gets up and walks out of shot.*
Shot 236.
Medium long shot of DENSON, *frowning, as* ROWNTREE
walks past him towards the door.
Shot 237.
Medium long shot, low angle, of ROWNTREE *opening the*
door.
ROWNTREE *shouting* : Phillips!
Shot 238.
Medium shot from above of DENSON *still seated. He is*
apprehensive.
DENSON : Oh, for God's sake, Rowntree.
Shot 239.
Medium long shot from below as ROWNTREE *turns away*
from the door to look quizzically in DENSON's *direction.*
*Shot 240. (Black and white stock, magenta tint.)
Cut to the Boot Room. High angle close-up of MACHIN
emptying a can of beans into a saucepan on a small stove.
He moves over to a frying pan in which sausages, eggs
and bacon are sizzling. Some BOYS *laugh excitedly, off.*
BRUNNING *off* : Come on, Machin! We're waiting.
MACHIN : Right—Biles' is ready—here.
*Shot 241.
Medium long shot of the group of shirt-sleeved SCUM.
MACHIN *forks* BILES' *egg from the frying pan.* BRUNNING,
JUTE *and* BOBBY PHILLIPS *look on. (Still on page 43)*
BILES : Mm. Lovely.
MACHIN *stands up, with* BRUNNING *sitting on his left.*
BRUNNING : Hey, watch mine. The big one. Big one in the
middle.
BRUNNING, BILES *and* BOBBY PHILLIPS *all help them-*
selves to eggs, sausages and rashers of bacon from the
pan.
*Shot 242.
Medium close-up of a junior BOY *putting his head round*
the door.

72

BOY *urgently* : Phillips, Phillips—you're wanted! Rowntree!
He disappears.
*Shot 243.
As 241 : MACHIN, JUTE, BILES, BRUNNING *and* PHILLIPS,
all eating and chattering. PHILLIPS *makes a face,
swallows some bacon, puts down his plate and walks off.*
Shot 244. (Return to colour.)
High angle medium long shot of PHILLIPS *outside the
Whips' Common Room door. He pauses for a moment,
straightens his tie and smooths down his hair, and then
knocks on the door.*
Shot 245.
Back view of ROWNTREE *in close-up, waiting behind the
door inside the Common Room.*
ROWNTREE : Come in.
PHILLIPS *comes in and stands by the door, impassive.*
Shot 246.
High angle medium shot of FORTINBRAS *and* BARNES
looking expectantly towards them.
Shot 247.
Medium shot of PHILLIPS *who stands, waiting.*
ROWNTREE *goes up to him.* PHILLIPS *closes the door.*
ROWNTREE *looks at* DENSON *with quiet mockery.*
ROWNTREE : Well?
Shot 248.
Medium shot of DENSON. *He shows no reaction.*
Shot 249.
Medium shot of PHILLIPS, *seen past* ROWNTREE.
ROWNTREE *to* PHILLIPS : You'll be scumming for Denson from
now on. *To* DENSON : All right with you, Richard?
Shot 250.
Medium shot of BARNES *and* FORTINBRAS *grinning at*
DENSON.
Shot 251.
Medium shot from above of DENSON *registering mingled
embarrassment and anger. He takes refuge behind his
newspaper again.*
Shot 252.
Medium shot of ROWNTREE.

73

ROWNTREE *to* PHILLIPS : Very well. You may go.

PHILLIPS *turns and leaves the room, his lips slightly pursed. Camera pans with* ROWNTREE *as he takes a step in* DENSON'S *direction. He looks down at him, with quiet irony.*

ROWNTREE : Say thank you.

Shot 253.

Music. Cut to JOHNNY'S *study. It is very like* MICK'S, *but with warmer colours. The walls are covered with pictures of girls—models, pin-ups and nudes. Detail shot of bookshelves: misty,* Vogue-*like glamour pictures.*

Shot 254.

Music out. Medium shot of JOHNNY *sitting on the couch leafing through a copy of* Woman's Own.

JOHNNY : Aries. That's Mick. *Reads :* ' No matter how strong the urge, resist any temptation to go into battle this month.' *Camera tracks back and* MICK *comes into shot, lounging in an armchair: in the background, Czech students marching over the Charles Bridge in Prague. He is writing in a notebook with a red pen. He listens as* JOHNNY *continues to read :* ' Otherwise you run the risk of not only being on the wrong side, but possibly in the wrong war.' *He chuckles.* So now you know.

MICK *picks up a bottle of vodka and takes a swig.*

MICK : The whole world will end very soon—black brittle bodies peeling into ash.

Camera tracks further back, then pans as MICK *hands the bottle to* WALLACE *who is sitting opposite.* WALLACE *takes a swig and turns to a mirror in front of him.* MICK *and* JOHNNY *are now out of shot. He examines his hair-line.*

WALLACE *moodily* : I'm going bald. It must be something they put in the soup. I'll look senile before I even leave this dump. *There is a chuckle, off.*

Shot 255.

Medium close-up of JOHNNY *reading from another page.*

JOHNNY *reading* : ' My husband seems to feel it's all right to make love anywhere in the house.'

Shot 256.

High angle medium close-up of MICK.

74

JOHNNY *off, reading* : ' I cannot agree; surely the bedroom is the right and only place for this very private happening.' JOHNNY *chuckles.*
> *There is the sound of heavy breathing, off.*
> *Shot 257.*
> *Medium close-up of* WALLACE *breathing into his cupped hands and sniffing. (Still on page 44)*
WALLACE : Have I got bad breath?
MICK *off* : There's no such thing as a wrong war.
> *Shot 258.*
> *Medium shot from above of* JOHNNY *reading, with* MICK *lounging back in the foreground. His notebook is on his knees.*
MICK : Violence and revolution are the only pure acts.
JOHNNY : Do you know—in Calcutta somebody dies of starvation every eight minutes.
MICK : Eight minutes is a long time.
> JOHNNY *tosses his magazine aside, and picks up another.*
> *Shot 259.*
> *Medium close-up of* WALLACE *still trying to smell his own breath.*
WALLACE : Every morning I wake up dreaming I've got bad breath. My whole body's rotting. *He drinks from the vodka bottle.*
MICK *off* : War is the last possible creative act.
> *Shot 260.*
> *Medium long shot of* JOHNNY *looking at another magazine.* MICK *snaps his note book shut, and puts it on the table beside him.* JOHNNY *comes over and shows* MICK *a full-page picture of a naked girl.*
JOHNNY : Isn't she beautiful?
MICK *taking the picture* : Hello, sweetheart . . . *He kisses it.*
> *Camera pulls back as* WALLACE *comes into shot, dragging his chair over to* MICK *and* JOHNNY.
MICK : There's only one thing you can do with a girl like this. Walk naked into the sea together as the sun sets, make love once . . . then die.
JOHNNY *sighing* : Fan-tas-tic!
> WALLACE *takes the picture and gazes at it a moment.*

75

(Still on page 44) Then he licks it. MICK *and* JOHNNY *look at him, amused, as he strokes the photograph.*

WALLACE : What makes me nervous about girls is, you never know what they're thinking.

JOHNNY : I don't think they *do* think.

MICK *turns sharply.*

MICK : Hey—quick!

He snatches the vodka bottle away and hides it under a cupboard next to him. WALLACE *turns his chair forward and* JOHNNY *and* MICK *look casual.*[1]

Shot 261.

Medium shot of DENSON *coming through the study door and closing it behind him. Camera tracks back to medium long shot, revealing* WALLACE, JOHNNY *and* MICK *all looking at him.*

DENSON : You've been drinking alcohol.

MICK : No, we haven't.

DENSON : Where's the bottle?

WALLACE : What bottle?

DENSON : Breathe.

Shot 262.

Close-up of WALLACE, *still seated. He pokes his tongue out with a polo mint on the tip. He breathes heavily at* DENSON.

Shot 263.

Medium shot of DENSON, *who is getting angry.*

DENSON : Stand up when a Whip's in your study! *They all stand up reluctantly.* Get your hands out of your pockets. Your hair's too long, all of you. You'll have a two-minute cold shower tomorrow morning. *He notices the necklace of teeth which* MICK *is wearing round his neck. To* MICK : What in hell are those?

Shot 264.

Medium close-up of MICK, *past* DENSON *who has his back to camera.* JOHNNY *stands behind* MICK.

MICK : They're my teeth. They're my good luck.

DENSON *disgustedly* : There's still blood on them. They're a

---

[1] End of reel two.

breeding ground for bacteria. *He rips the string of teeth from round* MICK'S *neck.* I'm confiscating them. *He turns towards the door.*

Shot 265.

Medium long shot of DENSON, *looking back at them.*

DENSON : You're a degenerate, Travis.

He goes out and closes the door.

Shot 266.

Medium close-up of MICK *looking after him, with* JOHNNY *in medium shot behind him.*

Shot 267.

Cut to a long shot of the House. It is morning, and a bell rings off.

Shot 268.

Low angle long shot of DENSON'S *bedroom window. The bell is still ringing. Sounds of voices, feet shuffling, a door slamming.*

Shot 269.

The inside of DENSON'S *room. Medium shot as* BOBBY PHILLIPS *comes through the door carrying a bowl of water and a towel. A photograph of the Queen is visible on the wall behind him. Camera pans and tracks back as he walks over to the bed where* DENSON *is lying, still asleep. There is a recruiting advertisement on the wall above his bed, and a picture of Glamis Castle.* PHILLIPS *puts the bowl down by the bed and opens the curtains.*

Shot 270.

Medium close-up from above of DENSON *in bed. One eye opens and follows* PHILLIPS *as he comes over to the bed again.*

Shot 271.

Low angle medium close-up of PHILLIPS' *hands lathering a shaving-brush. Camera tilts up to a medium close-up of his face as he looks away, out of the window—very cool and blond.*

Shot 272.

Medium close-up of DENSON. *He raises himself on to one elbow and gropes for his glasses, finds them and puts them on. Camera eases up with him.* PHILLIPS *comes into shot*

77

and starts to lather Denson's *face.* Denson *does not look up: his feelings can be felt, not seen.*
Shot 273.
The Shower Room. Long shot of Boys *in the line of shower cubicles, and others waiting to shower, or drying themselves. There is plenty of activity, the air is full of steam and the* Boys *are shouting and singing.* Johnny *stands in the furthest shower, right of screen, with* Mick *and* Wallace *leaning against the washbasins on the right-hand wall, waiting for their turn.* Peanuts *comes into shot, followed by* Stephans, *who studiously ignores* Mick *and* Wallace, *hangs up his dressing gown and goes into another shower. (Still on page 61)*
Shot 274.
Medium shot of Stephans *going into his shower, passing* Jones *and* Fisher *in their respective cubicles. Camera pans with him, and continues until it reaches* Johnny, *who is gritting his teeth under the cold punishment shower.*

Denson *off*: Right! Knightly, out . . .
Shot 275.
Medium shot from above of Denson *seated back to camera, waist-deep in a large, old-fashioned bath, holding a stop-watch. He shouts over his shoulder as* Fisher *passes in the foreground.*

Denson: Wallace, get under!
Shot 276.
Medium shot of Johnny *coming out of the shower:* Mick *hands him his towel.* Wallace *takes off his Judo-robe and goes into the shower.*
Shot 277.
Denson *turns back, in high angle medium shot, and continues to wash himself.*
Shot 278.
High angle medium close-up of Wallace *gasping under the shower.*
Shot 279.
Medium shot as Phillips *comes through from the changing room with a cup of tea on a tray. Camera pans with*

him as he crosses without enthusiasm to stand beside
Denson *in the bath.* Phillips *hands him the tea;*
Denson *helps himself to sugar. (Still on page 61)*
Shot 280.
Medium shot of two Boys, *one of them* Graves, *under*
showers. Keating *comes over and changes places with the*
other Boy *as* Graves *looks round his partition, and*
laughs.
Shot 281.
Medium close-up of Wallace *in his shower.*
Denson *off* : Right . . .
Shot 282.
High angle medium close-up of Denson. *He looks up*
from his tea . . .
Denson : Wallace, out. Travis, get in.
Shot 283.
Medium shot of Mick *and* Johnny, *with* Wallace *in*
the shower cubicle. Mick *and* Wallace *change places.*
Mick *stands provokingly on the edge of the jet of water.*
Shot 284.
Medium close-up of Denson *looking over in* Mick's
direction, tea-cup in hand.
Denson : Go on—in the middle.
Shot 285.
Medium shot of Mick, *with* Wallace *and* Johnny *in*
medium shot outside his shower cubicle. Mick *shuffles*
through to the back of the shower.
Denson *off* : Back a bit ! Mick *shuffles back, back to camera,*
Forward a bit ! Mick *ends up under the main force of the*
shower.
Shot 286.
High angle medium close-up of Denson, *who has turned*
back, drinking his tea. Phillips *is still standing by the*
bath holding the tray.
Shot 287.
Medium close-up of Mick *under the shower, back to*
camera. His back muscles flutter uncontrollably under the
ice-cold water. After a time he turns very slowly towards
Denson.

Shot 288.
Medium long shot as DENSON *climbs out of the bath, back to camera. Camera pans and holds as* PHILLIPS *holds out his bathrobe for him to put on.*
Shot 289.
Medium close-up of MICK *looking furiously in* DENSON'S *direction.*
MICK *through clenched teeth* : My time's up, you bastard.
Shot 290.
Medium shot of DENSON *walking towards camera.* PUSSY GRAVES *passes him in the foreground.*
DENSON : Stay there until I get back. *He goes out.*
Shot 291.
MICK *turns again under the shower. The camera creeps in as the water continues to beat down on his head and his hunched back.*
Fade out.

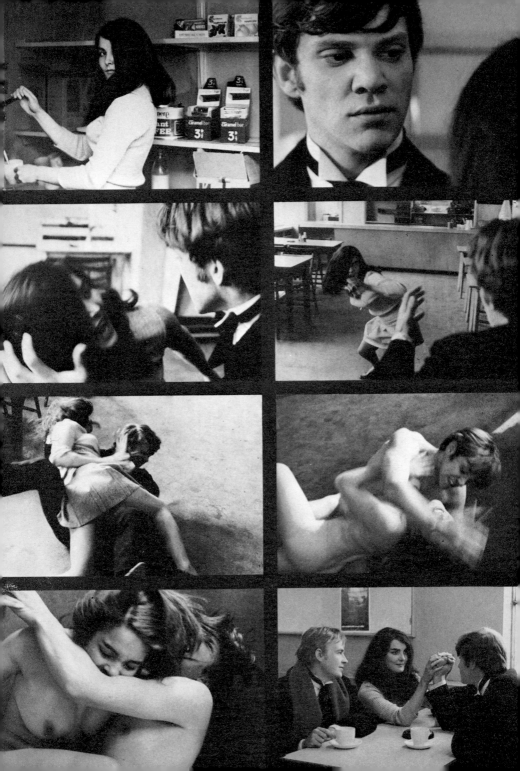

4

Shot 292. Title : RITUAL AND ROMANCE
Fade out.
Shot 293.
Fade in on a long shot of the College buildings from the playing fields, goal posts in the foreground. It is morning. We hear the Boys *finishing a psalm in the Chapel.*
School *singing, off* : ' Glory be to the Father, and to the Son,
And to the Holy . . .'
Shot 294.
Interior of the Chapel. Low angle shot of a stained glass window.
School *singing, off* : '. . . Ghost,
As it was in the . . .'
*Shot 295. (Black and white stock, magenta tint.)
Long shot of Rowntree *walking up the aisle, every inch a leader,* Boys *standing in the pews on either side.*
School *singing* : '. . . beginning,
Is now and ever shall be,
World without end,
Amen.'
Camera pans with Rowntree *as he walks into medium close-up and goes out of shot. The music ends.*
*Shot 296.
High angle long shot of the congregation of Boys *and the* Chaplain *and* Choir *all sitting down noisily.*
Rowntree *off* : The Book of Deuteronomy, chapter four, the first verse . . . *Coughing, off.*
*Shot 297.
Low angle medium shot of Rowntree, *reading the lesson from a large bible on the lectern. He speaks gravely, sternly. (Still on page 62)*
Rowntree : ' Now therefore hearken, O Israel, unto the statutes and unto the judgements which I teach you . . .'
*Shot 298.
High angle medium long shot of Boys *seated in the pews.*

MICK *is in the foreground: he looks at* ROWNTREE, *unimpressed.*

ROWNTREE *off:* ' That ye may live and go in and possess the land, which the Lord God of your Fathers giveth unto you.'

*Shot 299.

Low angle medium close-up of ROWNTREE.

ROWNTREE : ' Ye shall not add unto the word which I command you, neither shall ye diminish ought from it.'

*Shot 300.

Medium shot of MR. STEWART: *his eyelids droop heavily with fatigue—or disenchantment? Along the row* MR. THOMAS *twiddles his moustache, thoughtfully.*

ROWNTREE *off:* ' That ye keep the commandments of the Lord your God, which I command you. Behold, I have taught you statutes and judgements even as the Lord my God commanded me . . .'

*Shot 301.

Cut back to ROWNTREE *in medium close-up.*

ROWNTREE : ' Keep therefore and do them. For this is your wisdom and your understanding in the sight of the nations . . .'

*Shot 302.

High angle medium shot of MICK. *He looks away, up at the windows opposite. (Still on page 62)*

ROWNTREE *off:* '. . . which shall hear all these statutes and say, surely this nation is a wise and understanding people.'

Shot 303. (Return to colour.)

Low angle medium shot of a stained glass window: St. Michael drawing his sword.

ROWNTREE *off* : Here endeth the lesson.

A whistle blows shrilly, off.

*Shot 304. (Black and white stock, magenta tint.)

Low angle medium close-up of BARNES *in the gymnasium. Camera pans right as he walks across to the vaulting-box.*

BARNES : Right, through vault. Biles !

*Shot 305.

Long shot of BILES *and other* BOYS *lining up at the other end of the gym.* BARNES *has positioned himself in the foreground by the box.* BILES *runs forward and vaults over, followed by the others.*

86

BARNES *instructing* : Feet together! Right, good. Good. It's a *through* vault, Machin. Right.

*Shot 306.

Medium close-up of BARNES *easing the* BOYS *over as they vault over the box.*

BARNES : Come on, keep your head up. Head up!

*Shot 307.

BARNES : Come on, more effort. More effort, Phillips. Come on!

Medium shot of the queue of BOYS *waiting their turn,* JUTE *at the end, looking anxious. The* BOYS *gradually move up to vault until only* JUTE *and two others are left.*

*Shot 308.

Medium shot of BARNES *as the last boy before* JUTE *does the jump.*

BARNES : A bit more push-up. Good. Jute, come *on*!

*Shot 309.

Long shot of JUTE. *He hesitates, is about to move forward, hesitates again.*

BARNES *off* : Come on, Jute. *He claps his hands.* Jute! Come on!

JUTE *finally takes the plunge and runs towards the vaulting-box.*

*Shot 310.

Medium long shot of BARNES *standing by the box.* JUTE *comes into shot at a run and heaves himself at the box, crashing awkwardly and heavily, straddled across it.*

JUTE *winded* : Oooh!

BARNES *grabs* JUTE *impatiently by the pants and hauls him over.*

*Shot 311.

Low angle medium close-up of BARNES *heaving him over.*

BARNES : All right.

*Shot 312.

Medium shot of BARNES *standing by the file of boys.* JUTE *trots over to join them. Pan with* BARNES *as he moves across the gym, blowing his whistle.*

BARNES : Right, all of you on your toes. Get your sweaters.
He blows the whistle again, and the boys start to run out to the right.
*Shot 313.
Medium shot of the BOYS *running towards the door, followed by* BARNES.
*Shot 314. (Black and white stock, change to ' rose ' tint.)
Cut to the gallery above the gym. Medium shot of the BOYS *coming through the door on the left, still running.*
BARNES *off* : Get your sweaters.
Camera pans with BILES *and holds as he stops to pick up his sweater, followed by* PHILLIPS *and* MACHIN. *Music begins. Camera tracks with* PHILLIPS *as he walks towards the balustrade. (Still on page 63)*
*Shot 315.
High angle shot from PHILLIPS' *point of view. Camera tracks up to the gallery balustrade in the foreground: over it we see* WALLACE *on the floor below, preparing to use the high bar. He is bent over, rubbing his hands with resin from a box on the floor. He looks up. (Still on page 63)*
*Shot 316.
Medium shot from below. BILES *and* MACHIN *watch from the gallery;* PHILLIPS *stands on their left.*
*Shot 317.
High angle medium shot of WALLACE *rubbing his hands with resin. Camera follows him as he stands under the bar. He turns round, and grins broadly. (Still on page 63) He turns back.*
*Shot 318.
Low angle medium close-up of PHILLIPS. *He watches, transfixed.*
*Shot 319.
High angle medium shot from PHILLIPS' *viewpoint, as* WALLACE *grips the bar. He pulls himself up and starts to swing.*
*Shot 320.[1]
High angle long shot. WALLACE *swings up and over the*

---

[1] Shots 320 to 324 all in slow motion.

bar. *He circles it with arms fully extended. Speed slightly slowed.*
Shot 321.
Low angle medium close-up of PHILLIPS. *He begins to put on his sweater, also in slow motion. His gaze remains fixed on* WALLACE.
Shot 322.
High angle shot, now closer, of WALLACE *swinging on the bar.*
Shot 323.
Low angle medium close-up of PHILLIPS *pulling his sweater down over his face. He still stares down, as in an intense dream. (Still on page 63)*
Shot 324.
High angle shot of WALLACE. *(Still on page 63) A last full circle, then he flies, somersaulting, off the bar and out of frame. A moment of emptiness.*
Shot 325.
Low angle medium close-up of PHILLIPS. *(Still on page 63) With an instinctive gesture he brushes his hair aside, then stands, looking down at the empty bar, still in an intense dream. The music stops.*

BARNES *off*: Back to the House. Hup! Hup! Out you go! Up, up, up, up! Come on, Phillips.

Boys in sweaters pass at a jog behind PHILLIPS. *He is jerked back to reality, turns and runs out of frame.* BARNES' *voice continues.*
Shot 326. (Black and white stock, change back to magenta tint.)
Overhead long shot of the gym. JOHNNY *is lunging forward with a fencing foil.* WALLACE *rushes into shot, grabs a foil from the wall and begins to fence with* JOHNNY.
Shot 327.
Low angle medium close-up of WALLACE, *past a close-up of* JOHNNY. *The shot favours* WALLACE. *Both are laughing excitedly. Camera pans as* WALLACE *jumps teasingly, and then ducks behind the punch bag trying to hide from* JOHNNY.

89

*Shot 328.

Low angle long shot of MICK *swinging down on a climbing rope. Camera tilts up as he swings over.*

MICK : War!

*Shot 329.

Low angle medium close-up of MICK, *swinging back. He jumps from the rope.*

*Shot 330.

Medium shot of WALLACE *and* JOHNNY *running in to challenge* MICK *as he lands on the floor.*

MICK : War . . .

*Shot 331.

MICK *stands on guard in medium shot. Camera pans as* MICK *parries to his left and then to his right.*

MICK : Even to the knife!

JOHNNY *off* : England . . .

*Shot 332.

Medium long shot of MICK *past* WALLACE. *They begin to duel, with ferocity and flamboyant style.*

JOHNNY *off* : . . . awake!

JOHNNY *leaps into shot and challenges* MICK *from the other side. Camera pans as* MICK *lunges towards him, and pans the other way as he goes for* WALLACE, *flicking his foil out of his hand. They are all whooping and shouting.*

*Shot 333.

Medium long shot of WALLACE *standing momentarily motionless as* MICK *has his foil at his throat.*

WALLACE : Give me another horse!

He dodges away to retrieve his weapon as MICK *swings round to* JOHNNY *who has come to the rescue from behind.*

*Shot 334.

Medium close-up of MICK *fencing ferociously. He is forced back, and runs out of frame, pursued by* JOHNNY.

MICK : We are not cotton-spinners all . . .

*Shot 335.

MICK : Some love England and her honour yet!

MICK *jumps on to the wall bars, and hangs by one hand*

90

in medium long shot, seen from below. He fights
JOHNNY *off, but loses his foil.* WALLACE *runs in, with a*
shout. Camera pans with MICK *as he swings hand over*
hand along the wall bars and tilts up as he climbs higher
to get out of their way. Hold as WALLACE *pins* MICK *to*
the wall with his foil against his chest. MICK'S *foil*
is thrown back into shot by JOHNNY, *and he catches it*
by the hilt one-handed.
**Shot 336.*
Medium long shot as MICK *and* JOHNNY *fence back.*
MICK *is driven against the vaulting-box.* WALLACE
jumps up on to the box and stands poised for the attack.
JOHNNY *jumps away again and* MICK *backs off.*
WALLACE : Death to tyrants!
WALLACE *leaps down from the box.*
**Shot 337.*
Low angle medium close-up of WALLACE *and* JOHNNY
running fast. Camera pans and tracks with them as they
close in on MICK, *fighting him back into the corner.*
MICK *duelling with gay abandon* : What stands if freedom
falls? Who dies if freedom lives? Ha! Ha!
MICK *opens the door behind him with one hand and*
slips through it, hotly pursued by JOHNNY *and* WALLACE.
Shot 338. (Return to colour.)
Crash of music. The empty fives court, dark walls and
dusty red floor. The door flings open: MICK *runs in,*
leaps and turns to face WALLACE *and* JOHNNY *in pursuit.*
(Still on page 64) Camera tracks back and pans as MICK
and WALLACE *fence until* MICK *is back up against the*
wall and JOHNNY *comes into shot. Pan and track in as*
MICK *breaks free with a cry and runs off to the right.*
JOHNNY *turns, runs, engages* MICK *again.* WALLACE *joins*
him in the attack. Camera closes in as MICK *is driven into*
a corner. MICK *breaks free again: camera tracks and pans*
as he and WALLACE *fight fiercely down the wall, till* MICK
is cornered again at the other end of the court. WALLACE
and JOHNNY *close in on him; with heavy, remorseless*
strokes they drive him to his knees. His foil clatters away
as it is flicked from his exhausted grasp.

91

Shot 339.

Medium close-up : MICK *crouches panting in the corner,* WALLACE'S *foil at his throat. He looks at his wrist, then turns it towards the others. Blood trickles down the palm.* MICK'S *eyes shine strangely. (Still on page 64)*

MICK : Blood! Real blood!

Shot 340.

Close-up of the portrait of the College Founder, with that shrewd Tudor look. In the background the usual sounds of the BOYS *assembled for a meal can be heard—clattering of cutlery, plates, and general chatter and laughter.*

Shot 341.

Medium long shot of MICK *holding a chair for* MRS. KEMP, *with exaggerated politeness. She sits at the head of the table; other* BOYS *are sitting on either side.* MICK *sits down on the right.*

Shot 342.

Medium close-up from above of MATRON'S *hand ladling out a brown stew from a massive bowl. She ladles gravy and anonymous lumps of meat onto a plate being held by a* BOY. *The* BOY *moves on, carrying his tray, and another tray comes into frame, held out for* MATRON *to fill the plates.*

Shot 343.

Medium close-up of MATRON *licking her lips, seen past a* BOY *half visible in close-up. She watches the* BOYS' *faces as one moves off and the next comes in. She goes on doling out the stew, smiling all the time.*

Shot 344.

MICK *and* JOHNNY *are sitting next to each other at the end of the Senior table in medium long shot.* WALLACE *sits opposite them, right of camera, and* MRS. KEMP *is between them at the head, back to camera.*

JOHNNY : Water, Mrs. Kemp?

Shot 345.

Medium close-up of MRS. KEMP *facing camera, looking vaguely in* JOHNNY'S *direction. He pours a glass of water out of shot.*

Shot 346.

As shot 344. JOHNNY *hands a glass of water to* MRS. KEMP, *seen from behind. All three boys are staring intently at her, not insolently, but disconcertingly.*

JOHNNY : Lovely day, Mrs. Kemp.

WALLACE *holds the salt pot.*

WALLACE : Salt, Mrs. Kemp? *Reaching for a dish of greens :* Spring greens, Mrs. Kemp?

MICK *smiling pleasantly :* Dead Man's leg today, Mrs. Kemp. *He grasps a bottle of Dad's Sauce and holds it out to her. Do* you need this, Mrs. Kemp?

Shot 347.

Medium close-up of MRS. KEMP *looking at the sauce bottle being thrust at her. Her hand rises involuntarily and hovers in front of her breasts. (Still on page 81)*

MRS. KEMP *with a faint smile :* No, thank you. MICK *puts down the bottle.*

The desk bell rings off.

ROWNTREE *off :* Quiet.

MRS. KEMP *looks off, left.*

Shot 348.

Medium close-up of WALLACE *on one side of the table, seen from above, with* JOHNNY *and* MICK *on the other side in medium shot. They all look off, left of camera,* WALLACE *casual,* MICK *and* JOHNNY *not co-operative.*

ROWNTREE *off :* Cheering at College matches has degenerated completely. This will cease. The House will attend the match this afternoon and cheer. Loudly.

Shot 349.

The playing fields: loud cheering. Long shot of a line of spectators lined up along the touchlines, boys, masters and wives. Camera pans along the line until it reaches a scrum. Left of screen the College team, in blue jerseys with white and red stripe round the chest; opponents in green jerseys. The College scrum-half gets the ball out of the scrum and throws it back to his three-quarter line. Movement with the ball left to right until the College three-quarter is brought down; zoom in to loose scrum. Greens get the ball back, then sweep forward right to

*left until their man is driven into touch. The spectators
break back, still cheering; the players run up for the
line-out.* WALLACE *is the touch-judge.*
Shot 350.
Medium close-up of WALLACE *marking the throw-in.*
Shot 351.
*Medium long shot of the throw-in. The ball is thrown
towards camera over the players' heads; College gets the
ball and sweeps forward left to right, camera panning
with them.*
Shot 352.
Zoom shot, tightening on MATRON *at the touchline,
cheering as the players sweep past. She calls out savagely,
with clenched fist.*
MATRON : Fight! Fight! Fight, College, Fight! Fight! Fight!
Shot 353.
*High angle long shot of a busy road in the town: in the
centre of frame a grass ' island ', vivid green against the
dark tarmac. Sounds of cheering mix into traffic noise.
We see* MICK *and* JOHNNY *running together, linked with
a pair of handcuffs. They are wearing dark overcoats;*
MICK *has his black scarf,* JOHNNY, *one of dark red.
Camera zooms in as they cross the road to the island,
dodging the traffic. They dodge past a couple of corpora-
tion gardeners, then hurry on, camera tilting down and
right as* MICK *holds up his hand imperiously, forcing a
scarlet sports car to screech to a halt. Camera tilts down
as they walk on to the road in the foreground.* JOHNNY
stumbles: MICK *drags him up. The traffic noise dies.
Silence, then delicate music.*
Shot 354.
The window of a silversmith's shop.
Shot 355.
*A lingerie shop-window, full of bras, corsets, and
stockings.*
Shot 356.
*A dress shop-window, with elegant, statuesque models.
The music stops and the traffic can be heard again. The
town is busy with Saturday afternoon shoppers.*

Shot 357.

Long shot from the opposite side of the street of MICK *and* JOHNNY *walking along a pavement.* JOHNNY *stops to look in a window.* MICK *pretends to threaten* JOHNNY *with a razor; they stand for a moment as a bus passes in the foreground.* MICK *slashes; they fight, darting to and fro among the passers-by. The camera pans along the pavement with them. Hold as they fight:* MICK *lunges, grabs* JOHNNY *and manhandles him to the ground. Passers-by glance but make no move to enquire or interfere.* JOHNNY *writhes in agony on the pavement, then lies still with* MICK *standing over him triumphantly. A woman walks past, looks back at* JOHNNY, *and comes back to* MICK. *She looks at* MICK; *she looks at* JOHNNY; *she looks at* MICK *again.* MICK *looks at her.*

Shot 358.

A car showroom full of MG 1100s and MGBs. The traffic noise is replaced by the delicate music again.

Shot 359.

Medium shot of a Hillman Hunter in a showroom.

Shot 360.

Medium shot from above of rows of gleaming motor-cycles in another showroom.

Shot 361.

The music stops and the noise of the traffic creeps back. Close-up of MICK *staring intently through the show-room window. He is smoking a cigarette.*

Shot 362.

Repeat shot of the motor-bikes.

Shot 363.

MICK *and* JOHNNY, *seen from inside the motor-bike showroom, through the window, walk round to the entrance in medium long shot.* MICK *throws his cigarette away. Pan with them and hold as they walk through the door.*

Shot 364.

Medium long shot of a SALESMAN *sitting behind a desk at the other end of the showroom. Motor-bikes in front of him.*

Shot 365.

MICK *and* JOHNNY *inspect the bikes, seen in medium long shot.* MICK *looks at one row, and* JOHNNY *wanders off to look at others, in the background.*

Shot 366.

High angle medium shot of the SALESMAN. *He looks up suspiciously.*

Shot 367.

Medium close-up of MICK; *he grins at the* SALESMAN *then looks carefully at one of the bikes. He smiles reassuringly in the* SALESMAN'S *direction. Suddenly he swings his leg over the bike, and seats himself in the saddle.*

Shot 368.

Medium shot of MICK *astride the powerful red machine. He grips the handle-bars.* JOHNNY, *in long shot, is looking at another bike. Suddenly* MICK *kicks over the starter and revs up the engine. The noise reverberates through the quiet showroom.*

Shot 369.

Medium shot of the SALESMAN *looking up in alarm.*

Shot 370.

Medium close-up of JOHNNY *looking with amusement in* MICK'S *direction.*

Shot 371 .

Medium long shot as MICK *slides the bike off its stand and puts it into gear. He suddenly jerks forward, camera panning with him, and holding as he rides round towards the right and out of shot. The* SALESMAN *jumps up, waving his arms, and runs forward, dodging between the bikes.* JOHNNY *comes into shot, rushing after* MICK.

Shot 372.

Medium long shot of MICK *driving into the garage workshop, revving the engine all the time. Pan with him until he turns and then camera tracks back and pans as he rides past* JOHNNY, *almost runs over the* SALESMAN, *and roars round the garage.*

SALESMAN *off* : Stop ! Bring it back !

The SALESMAN *runs wildly out of shot, stumbling as he*

96

goes. MICK *rides on round the garage, past the crimson wall opposite, camera panning till he passes* JOHNNY *again.* MICK *whistles to him.*

Shot 373.

Medium shot of JOHNNY; *he runs towards the bike. Pan with him as he reaches* MICK *and climbs on to the back of the bike while it is still moving. Camera pans slightly as* MICK *accelerates and, in long shot, rides the bike out of the garage.*

Shot 374.

High angle close-up of the white lines in the middle of a road, camera tracking fast along them. Music crashes in. Camera tilts up and pans along the trees. The road stretches before us. The noise of the motorcycle comes in.

Shot 375.

Medium long shot of MICK *and* JOHNNY *bowling along a main road, towards camera, which tracks back with them.*

Shot 376.

Long shot: the road is winding up hill into the country. Trees and cows at pasture in the background. The bike rides up towards and past camera. Sunshine and rich green.

Shot 377.

Camera tracks along past trees and hedges:fields stretch away in the distance. Cars pass in the foreground.

Shot 378

MICK *and* JOHNNY *riding along, camera tracking with them. Camera tightens as they shout and laugh, their hair streaming back in the wind. The music broadens lyrically. (Still on page 81)*

Shot 379.

The countryside again. Trees, fields and hedgerows. The rich shade of a summer lane.

Shot 380.

Long shot from the centre of a grassy field: over the hedge the bike can be seen, speeding along the main road. By a signpost it slows down, turns left, and accele-

rates down a tree-shaded lane.
Shot 381.
Camera tracking along country lane: hedges and trees on either side. Camera tilts up to a low angle shot of trees and sky, blurring as they travel past.
Shot 382.
High angle long shot of MICK *and* JOHNNY *emerging from the lane on to a main road. The camera pans with them as they circle a roundabout at speed, then off up an arterial road. The music mixes into heavy traffic noise.*
Shot 383.
Cars and lorries going away from camera. The BOYS *on the bike come along the road towards camera. Camera zooms with them as they approach, panning left then right as they turn and drive past camera into the fore-court of a transport café. Bold lettering on the façade:*
PACKHORSE CAFE.
Shot 384.
Medium shot from behind as JOHNNY *gets off the bike and walks out of shot, looking towards the café.* MICK *slides the bike on to its stand and pats the petrol tank like a horse. He follows* JOHNNY.
*Shot 385. (Black and white stock, magenta tint.)
Long shot of the café looking towards the door from the counter. It is completely empty; tables line the left-hand wall. There is a jukebox in a recess on the right. JOHNNY *walks straight towards the counter.* MICK *stops for a moment and runs a comb through his hair in front of a mirror on the left-hand wall.*
*Shot 386.
Reverse long shot. JOHNNY *reaches the counter:* MICK *breaks from the mirror and joins* JOHNNY *at the counter. They lean forward.* MICK *knocks sharply on the counter. Music ends.*
*Shot 387.
Long shot through the serving hatch, to the kitchen behind. At first the frame is empty. Then a GIRL *appears: plain sweater, long dark hair, large dark eyes. She*

98

glances for a moment through the hatch, then carries on, the camera panning with her. She walks out of shot and camera continues to pan, picking up MICK *and* JOHNNY *with backs to camera. Camera pans back as the* GIRL *comes through the door from the kitchen, and walks along the counter in front of the* BOYS.

GIRL *bored* : Yes?

JOHNNY : Two coffees, please.

Pan continues as the GIRL *walks to the left end of the counter. She stops, looking back at them.*

GIRL : Black or white?

*Shot 388.

Medium shot of JOHNNY, *seen past* MICK.

JOHNNY : White.

Medium close-up of the GIRL *pouring coffee into cups. She is just about to fill the second cup.*

*Shot 389.

Medium close-up of MICK *with* JOHNNY *behind.*

MICK *challengingly* : Black.

*Shot 390.

Medium close-up of the GIRL. *She looks at him, meeting his challenge, puts the coffee jug down, turning away.*

*Shot 391.

Medium close-up of MICK, *with* JOHNNY *beyond him, seen from above. They both lean forward and look down over the counter.*

*Shot 392.

Medium close-up of the GIRL, *turned away from camera. She spoons some instant coffee into a cup from a large tin, then she pulls the lever on the urn and pours boiling water into the cup. The camera tilts down, dwelling on her hips and short skirt, then up again. She turns her head: one fierce dark eye is framed by her long hair. (Still on page 82)*

*Shot 393.

Medium shot of JOHNNY *and* MICK *leaning over the counter.* MICK *grins.*

*Shot 394.

Medium long shot of the GIRL, *past* MICK. *They stare*

*at each other for a moment. Then she puts his cup down,
and slides them both along the counter, Western-style.*
Mick *picks up his cup and strolls nonchalantly along the
counter to face her.* Johnny *watches.*
*Shot 395.
Medium close-up of* Mick, *staring fixedly in the* Girl's
direction. He speaks laconically.

Mick : Sugar.

*He looks down and then suddenly lunges forward,
towards the* Girl.
*Shot 396.
Medium shot of* Mick *from behind. He is leaning across
the counter and has grabbed the* Girl *round the neck,
kissing her roughly on the mouth.* Johnny *watches them.
The* Girl *struggles free; with a sturdy swing, she slaps*
Mick *fair and square across the face.*
*Shot 397.
Medium close-up of* Mick. *He looks at the* Girl, *without
comment.*
*Shot 398.
Close-up from above of* Mick's *hand as he heaps two
desert spoonfuls of sugar into his cup. He stirs it, and
throws the spoon back into the tin.*
*Shot 399.
After a pause,* Mick, *in medium shot, picks up his cup
and walks back towards a table half-way down the café,
followed by* Johnny, *who is seen from behind.*
*Shot 400.
Medium long shot of the* Girl; *without movement or
expression, she watches from behind the counter.*
*Shot 401.
Medium long shot of* Mick *and* Johnny *still going back
to their table.* Mick *puts his cup down and goes over
to the juke box.* Johnny *goes and sits down, his back
to camera.*
*Shot 402.
Medium shot of* Mick *at the juke box. He puts in a coin
and selects a record. The mechanism whirls and a record
starts to play. It is the ' Sanctus ' from the* Missa Luba.

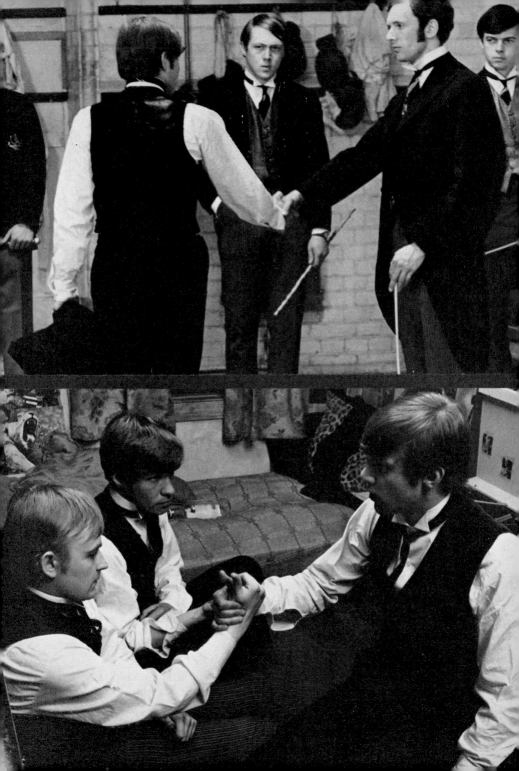

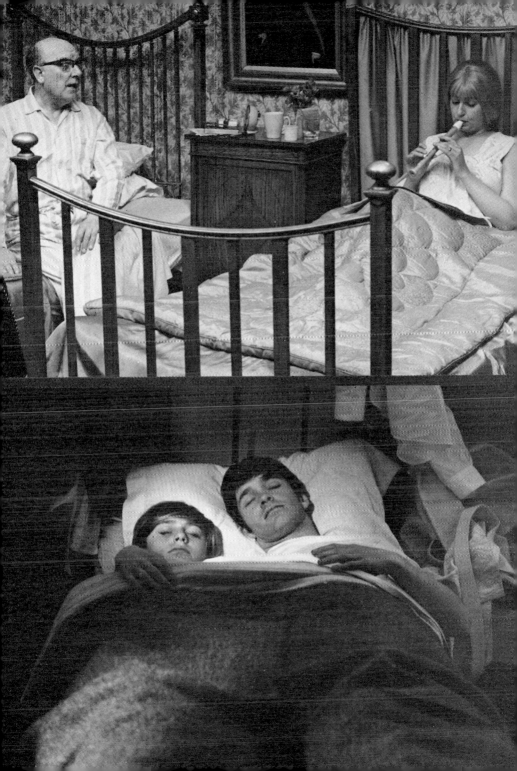

*Shot 403 .

High angle medium shot of JOHNNY seated at the table. He looks over to MICK with a faint smile, then leans forward and covers MICK's coffee cup with the saucer.
*Shot 404.

Medium shot of MICK leaning against the juke box, back to camera. The GIRL comes up behind him and slides her hand up over his shoulder. He turns round slowly.
*Shot 405.

Medium close-up of the GIRL, past MICK. Her look is steady, intense.

GIRL insistently: Go on, look at me.
*Shot 406.

Close-up of MICK, past the GIRL, right of picture. He looks down over her body, then raises his eyes to her face. (Still on page 82)

GIRL : I'll kill you. Look at my eyes.
*Shot 407.

Big close-up of the GIRL's eyes, seen from above over MICK's shoulder.

GIRL with slow intensity : Sometimes I stand in front of the mirror and my eyes get bigger and bigger, and I'm like a tiger. Pause. I like tigers. Suddenly she bares her teeth, tosses her hair, and snarls.
*Shot 408.

Close-up of MICK. He sniffs round the GIRL's face like an animal; then he suddenly hisses, lashing out at her with his nails. He lunges forward, growling, as if to bite her. (Still on page 82) The music rises in intensity and pitch.
*Shot 409 (Hand-held).

Medium shot as the GIRL retaliates. They snarl menacingly at each other, and circle round, the camera following their movements. MICK lashes out; the GIRL chases him back towards camera. They growl and spit. The GIRL comes at him, head lowered and hands out like claws. (Still on page 82) Camera retreats and pans with them as they edge along facing one another. The GIRL springs and they grapple: her teeth seem to be tearing at

105

his neck. MICK *breaks free, retreating. With a leap she is on him; he falls back; she is on top. The camera moves in as they wrestle furiously on the floor tearing, snarling and screaming. Drumming and chanting reach full volume. (Still on page 82)*
*Shot 410.
High angle medium close-up of MICK *and the* GIRL *naked on the floor. She sinks her teeth into* MICK'S *bare shoulder. He screams in pain. (Stills on page 82)*
*Shot 411.
Abruptly the music fades. High angle medium shot of JOHNNY *sitting placidly at the table drinking his coffee. The* GIRL, *fully dressed, comes into shot and passes behind him ruffling his hair. As she sits down next to him, camera tilts down with her.* MICK *appears and sits opposite them. He removes the saucer from his cup. Camera tracks round slightly to hold all three in shot.*
GIRL *smiling at* MICK : I like Johnny.
MICK *clicks his fingers and holds two out—silently indicating the start of a game.*
MICK : Scissors.
GIRL *holding out her clenched fist* : Stone.
MICK *opening his hand out flat* : Paper.
GIRL *holding out two fingers* : Scissors.
MICK *with clenched fist* : Stone.
The GIRL *slowly and sensually wraps his fist with her two hands. The 'Sanctus' gently starts again.*
GIRL : Paper. *(Still on page 82)*
*Shot 412. (Return to colour.)
A broad, green field: trees in the distance. Soft, lyrical atmosphere. Long shot as MICK *and* JOHNNY *circle the field on the motor bike; the* GIRL *stands between them, her hands on* MICK'S *shoulders, her hair blowing. The bike approaches camera: the* GIRL *raises her hands to lift her hair, then stretches her arms out wide. They laugh with joy. The camera tilts up as they ride out of shot. Hold sky and trees for a moment. Then picture and music fade.[1]*

---

[1] End of reel three.

106

5

Shot 413. TITLE :   DISCIPLINE
Fade out.
Shot 414.
High angle long shot of the Sweat Room, looking down through a window. It is night, and the BOYS *are sitting working at their desks.* ROWNTREE *walks slowly, impressively, invigilating. His footsteps echo heavily on the wooden boards.*
*Shot 415. (Black and white stock, magenta tint.)
The College buildings from the outside. Low angle shot of a lighted window. A dog barks somewhere in the distance.
Shot 416. (Return to colour.)
Very dark long shot of DENSON *in silhouette, his feet crunching on the gravel, as he checks doors and windows. Camera pans as he stops and looks down. He shines his torch suspiciously at something.*
Shot 417.
High angle medium close-up of MR. THOMAS, *startled, wriggling out from under a car, brandishing a spanner.*
MR. THOMAS : Anything wrong?
Shot 418.
Low angle close-up of DENSON *looking down at him.*
DENSON : No, it's all right, Sir, just duty rounds. *Pointedly.* You won't be long, will you, Sir?
MR. THOMAS *off* : Sorry, Denson, I didn't know it was so late.
Shot 419.
Medium close-up from above of MR. THOMAS *lying half under the car, blinking up into the torchlight.* DENSON *looks down, then walks off in front of him.*
DENSON : Good night, Sir.
MR. THOMAS : Good night, Denson.
The Chapel clock chimes.
Shot 420.
Cut to the school Armoury. It is dark. Low angle medium

shot of rifles stacked in racks along the wall.

PHILLIPS *off* : Now, if I pass . . .

Shot 421.

High angle close-up of WALLACE *leaning back over some wooden crates, smoking.*

PHILLIPS *off* : . . . all the tests, I'm definitely going to California.

Shot 422.

Medium close-up of PHILLIPS *past* WALLACE. *He is smoking a cigarette, rather inexpertly. (Still on page 83)*

PHILLIPS : I'm going to be a criminal lawyer. 'Course, it all takes about twenty years.

Shot 423.

Close-up of WALLACE, *from above.*

WALLACE *laughing* : We'll all be dead by then.

PHILLIPS *off* : Well, I believe in having a goal.

Shot 424.

Medium close-up of PHILLIPS, *past* WALLACE. *He drops his cigarette and stubs it out on the floor.*

PHILLIPS : That's the way you succeed. Actually, that's your trouble. You've no ambition.

Shot 425.

Medium shot from above of WALLACE *and* PHILLIPS. WALLACE *agrees good-temperedly and offers* PHILLIPS *another cigarette.*

WALLACE : I know . . . Your Mum coming for Founder's Day?

PHILLIPS *taking a cigarette* : Yes. She's bringing her new husband . . .

Shot 426.

Close-up of WALLACE, *intrigued.*

PHILLIPS *off* : . . . my new Dad.

WALLACE : What's he like?

PHILLIPS *off* : Actually, I don't think they're married.

Shot 427.

Medium close-up, from above, of PHILLIPS.

PHILLIPS *defiantly* : I don't care. I don't mind at all . . .

Shot 428.

Close-up of WALLACE, *serious.*

PHILLIPS *off* : . . . about that sort of thing.
> *Shot 429.*
> *Medium close-up of* PHILLIPS *puffing away at his cigarette. He is not so sure of himself.*

PHILLIPS : I shouldn't mind, should I?
> *Shot 430.*
> *Close-up of* WALLACE *looking at* PHILLIPS : *he is sympathetic, but these are deep waters.*

WALLACE : No. Oh, hell . . . I don't know.
> *Footsteps scrape on the gravel outside.* WALLACE *turns quickly.*
> *Shot 431.*
> *Medium close-up of* PHILLIPS *looking nervously towards the door.* WALLACE *jumps up and pulls him to his feet.*

WALLACE : Quickly! Out the back.
> *Shot 432.*
> *Medium long shot as* WALLACE *pushes* PHILLIPS *forward. Camera tracks back and pans with them.* PHILLIPS *slips through a gap in the wall, right of screen.*
> *Shot 433.*
> *Medium shot of the armoury door. It opens and* DENSON *comes in. He shines his torch round the armoury.*
> *Shot 434.*
> *Medium shot as* WALLACE *turns to face the glare.*
> *Shot 435.*
> DENSON *switches on the light, in medium shot.*

DENSON *sharply* : Can you explain yourself?
> *Shot 436.*
> *Medium shot of* WALLACE, *standing silently looking at him.*

DENSON *off* : What are you up to?

WALLACE : Nothing.
> *Shot 437.*
> *Close-up of* DENSON, *suspicious.*

DENSON : Who was with you?
> *Shot 438.*
> *Close-up of* WALLACE: *the faintest of smiles tinges his impassiveness.*

WALLACE : No one.

Shot 439.
Harsh music. A close-up of MICK'S *collage of violence.*
Shot 440.
Medium close-up of MICK, *his head inside a polythene bag. He is holding it down to make it airtight: as he breathes, it expands, then is sucked in horribly, clinging to the outlines of his face. After three breaths—in and out—he nods desperately.* JOHNNY'S *hand comes in to pull the bag off his head.*
Shot 441.
Medium long shot of MICK *fighting for breath; he is sitting cross legged on the couch in front of the window in his study.* JOHNNY *is next to him, kneeling up on the couch, a watch in his hand.* WALLACE *lounges in a chair against the wall, right of screen, turned towards* MICK *and* JOHNNY, *grasping a vodka bottle.*
JOHNNY : How did it feel?
MICK : Like drowning. *He leans back again and takes a deep breath.*
Shot 442.
Medium close-up of WALLACE, *thoughtfully drinking vodka from his bottle.*
Shot 443.
Medium long shot of MICK. *He comes in from the window and sits back;* JOHNNY *relaxes into the corner: above him a collage of animals and sport; a gorilla sitting in the pose of Rodin's ' Thinker '.*
JOHNNY : What's the most horrible way to die?
WALLACE : Mmm . . . getting a moth caught in your ear-drum . . .
Shot 444.
Medium close-up of WALLACE *holding the bottle on his knee.*
WALLACE : . . . you hear it as it eats into your brain.
MICK *off* : Being flayed alive.
Shot 445.
Medium long shot of MICK *and* JOHNNY, *past* WALLACE.
MICK : That's what the Crusaders did to their enemies. Used to send the neatly folded skins back to their victim's wives.

110

JOHNNY *after a pause* : Cancer's worse. My mother took six months. *A pause.*

MICK *leaning out of the window again* : The night's dead.

> *Shot 446.*
> *Medium close-up of* WALLACE. *His thoughts are elsewhere. He undoes his shirt and starts to scratch his chest sensually.*

MICK *off* : You can hardly breath outside. *Pause.* The thing I'd really hate is to have a nail banged through . . .

> *Shot 447.*
> *Medium long shot of* MICK *and* JOHNNY, *with* WALLACE *in the foreground.*

MICK : . . . the back of my neck. Slowly.

> *They look at each other as the absurdity of the idea grows on them. They begin to laugh. (Still on page 83)*

MICK *spluttering* : I don't see what difference the sp . . . speed makes . . .

> *Shot 448.*
> *Medium close-up of* WALLACE, *oblivious of the others, gently stroking his chest. The others can be heard giggling hysterically off.*

MICK *off* : The speed of the nail.

> *Shot 449.*
> *High angle medium long shot of* MICK *and* JOHNNY *rolling about helplessly as they laugh.* WALLACE *sits unmoved.* MICK *buries his head in an orange cushion, then sits back, laughing uncontrollably.*

JOHNNY *giggling* : Th-th-the nail's speed !

> *The camera tracks in and tilts down as* MICK *rolls off the couch on to the floor, clasping the cushion and doubled up with laughter,* JOHNNY *going out of shot. Hold in high angle medium shot as* JOHNNY *leans forward and* MICK *hits him with the cushion, both screaming with laughter.*
> *Shot 450.*
> *Close-up of* WALLACE *looking down over his shoulder at* MICK.
> *Shot 451.*
> *High angle shot of* MICK *lying on his back.* WALLACE'S

111

legs can also be seen. WALLACE *gets up quietly and goes over to the window.* JOHNNY *rocks backwards and forwards, laughing.* MICK, *still grasping his cushion, continues to gurgle uncontrollably.*

Shot 452.

Cut to MR. KEMP'S *private dining room—a small, high room with dark red wallpaper.* MR. KEMP *and the four* WHIPS *are seen in long shot, sitting round the table, in the centre of which a silver candelabra rises from an opulent mound of fruit. The meal is coming to an end.* MRS. KEMP, *standing, puts a decanter of port in front of* MR. KEMP *and then leaves the room in discreet silence.*

MR. KEMP : Thank you, my dear.

Camera begins a slow track in.

ROWNTREE : Of course, there's always a lunatic fringe. A . . . certain hard core in the studies.

MR. KEMP : Oh dear.

ROWNTREE : Yes.

   MR. KEMP *helps himself to port, and passes the decanter to* FORTINBRAS, *on his left. The* WHIPS *help themselves to fruit or nuts.*

ROWNTREE : We'll have to deal firmly with it in certain instances. *He cracks a nut.* It may be necessary to make a few examples.

MR. KEMP *nervously* : The Headmaster doesn't like too much thrashing.

ROWNTREE : He wouldn't like College to get a reputation for decadence.

DENSON : Hear, hear.

   The group are now in medium shot. DENSON *hands the decanter on to* BARNES.

MR. KEMP : Of course. Of course. And the Juniors, how are the Juniors?

ROWNTREE *blasé* : On the whole, dull.

MR. KEMP *hopelessly* : Oh dear.

ROWNTREE : Of course, it's just a . . .

   Shot 453.

   Low angle medium close-up of ROWNTREE, *past* DENSON.

112

The candles flicker at the bottom of frame.

ROWNTREE *continuing* : . . . matter of proportion. Unruly elements threaten the stability of the House. It's best to nip them in the bud.

Shot 454.

Medium shot of MR. KEMP, *nervously evasive.*

MR. KEMP : Yes. Well—you must do what you think best.

WHIPS *together* : Thank you, Sir.

Shot 455.

Medium close-up of ROWNTREE *sipping his glass of port.*

ROWNTREE, *with quiet superiority* : Thank you, Sir.

Shot 456.

Medium shot of MR. KEMP—*Pontius Pilate. He puts a large segment of orange in his mouth. He chews it, avoiding their eyes.*

BOYS *singing off* : ' Love so amazing . . .'

Shot 457.

Cut to a long shot of the empty corridor.

BOYS *singing off* : '. . . so divine . . .'

Shot 458.

Long shot of the Dining Room: the BOYS *at their tables, hymn books in their hands, singing the hymn for evening prayers.*

BOYS *singing* : '. . . Demands my heart, my life . . .'

Shot 459.

Low angle long shot of ROWNTREE, *with* MATRON *and* MRS. KEMP *on either side of him, behind the top table which is loaded with trays of buns, jugs of milk and cups.*

BOYS *singing* : '. . . my all ! '

ROWNTREE : The grace of our Lord, Jesus Christ, the love of God, and the fellowship of the Holy Ghost . . .

Shot 460.

Long shot of the BOYS *standing at the tables in varying degrees of attentiveness.*

ROWNTREE *off* : . . . be with us all, evermore, amen.

VOICE *off* : Senior table !

The Senior table files up to the top table, which is out of shot, headed by WALLACE, STEPHANS *and* MICK.

113

Shot 461.
Medium close-up of the table, with ROWNTREE, MATRON
and MRS. KEMP *on guard behind. Brown, sticky buns
shine, as hands hover and reach out for them; talk and
laughter.*
Shot 462.
High angle medium long shot of ROWNTREE, MATRON
and MRS. KEMP, *over the* BOYS' *heads.* ROWNTREE
*bangs the bell sharply. Everybody stops and looks up,
milling round the table.*
ROWNTREE : Quiet! As soon as you've finished, Juniors to the
Sweat Room, Seniors to their studies . . . and wait in silence.
He pauses to let this sink in. Carry on.
MRS. KEMP *suddenly* : Fisher!
Shot 463.
Medium close-up of MRS. KEMP *behind the table, with*
BOYS *standing in front of her.*
MRS. KEMP *furiously* : That's your second bun. I saw you!
Put it back!
Shot 464.
High angle long shot of the Sweat Room. The Junior
BOYS *are hurrying to their places, speculating excitedly
in low voices.* BRUNNING *stops; a small group questions
him.*
Shot 465.
PEANUTS' *study: the walls are covered with photographs
of planets, stars, the moon's surface. Colour pictures of
a baby in the womb.* PEANUTS *walks into frame and
camera tilts down as he sits at his desk.*
DENSON *shouting, off* : Travis! Wallace! Knightly!
PEANUTS *listens for a moment, then switches on the
desk light and pulls his microscope towards him.*
Shot 466.
Long shot of the House corridor. MICK, JOHNNY *and*
WALLACE *walk towards the* WHIPS' *room. Camera
pans as they pass. Hold as they reach the door.* MICK
knocks.
Shot 467.
Medium long shot of the WHIPS *grouped impressively in*

114

their room. BARNES *and* FORTINBRAS *are standing behind the table.* ROWNTREE *is propping himself up against it to confront the door, with* DENSON *sitting on his left. (Still on page 84)*

ROWNTREE : Come in. *The door opens.*

Shot 468.

Medium long shot of JOHNNY, MICK *and* WALLACE *as they come through the door, seen past* FORTINBRAS *on right of shot and* ROWNTREE *on the left, both back to camera.* MICK *closes the door, and steps in between* WALLACE *(camera left) and* JOHNNY.

ROWNTREE : Good evening. I imagine you know why you're here.

MICK *looks questioningly at* JOHNNY *and* WALLACE, *then back to* ROWNTREE.

MICK *innocently* : No.

Shot 469.

Medium long shot of ROWNTREE, *formal and dignified, with* BARNES *and* FORTINBRAS *behind.*

ROWNTREE : For being a nuisance. A general nuisance in the House.

Shot 470.

Medium shot of JOHNNY, MICK *and* WALLACE. *They look innocently puzzled. (Still on page 84)*

MICK : What do you mean—being a nuisance? What have we done?

Shot 471.

Medium close-up of ROWNTREE, *with* BARNES *and* FORTINBRAS *behind.*

ROWNTREE : Done? It's your general attitude. You know exactly what . . .

Shot 472.

Medium shot of JOHNNY, MICK *and* WALLACE. MICK *is keeping cool, but stubborn.*

ROWNTREE *off* : . . . I mean.

MICK : Attitude?

ROWNTREE *off* : And we've decided to beat you for it.

Shot 473.

Medium long shot of the group of WHIPS. ROWNTREE

is impassive. DENSON *comes forward.* BARNES *and* FOR-TINBRAS *still behind.*

DENSON *impatiently* : Stand up properly when the Head of House addresses you!

Shot 474.

Medium shot of JOHNNY, MICK *and* WALLACE. *They stir slightly.*

DENSON *disgustedly, off* : There's something indecent about you, Travis.

Shot 475.

Medium close-up of DENSON; BARNES *lounges behind him.*

DENSON : The way you slouch about. You think we don't notice you with your hands in your pockets. The way you just *sit* there . . .

Shot 476.

Medium close-up of MICK. *He gives no ground.*

DENSON *off* : . . . looking at everyone.

ROWNTREE *off* : You three . . .

Shot 477.

Medium close-up of ROWNTREE: *he wants to bring this to an end.*

ROWNTREE : . . . have become a danger to the morale of the whole House.

Shot 478.

Medium close-up of MICK. *He looks down: his mouth twists scornfully.*

DENSON *furiously, off* : You can take that cheap little grin off your mouth!

Shot 479.

Medium close-up of DENSON. *He points to the badge on his blazer.*

DENSON : ' I serve the nation.'

Shot 480.

Medium shot of JOHNNY, MICK *and* WALLACE. MICK *looks insolent.*

DENSON *off* : You haven't the slightest idea what it means, have you? To you it's just one bloody joke.

MICK : Do you mean that bit of wool on your tit?

116

Shot 481.

Medium shot of ROWNTREE, *with* BARNES, DENSON *and* FORTINBRAS *behind him. He steps forward from the table.*

ROWNTREE : You're in the sixth form now. You should be prepared to set an example of responsibility.

BARNES *superciliously* : You're a nuisance.

DENSON : Pathetic.

ROWNTREE : And as such, you must be punished.

Shot 482.

Medium shot of JOHNNY, MICK *and* WALLACE.

ROWNTREE *off* : Well? Have you anything to say, any of you?

WALLACE *looks at* MICK, *while* JOHNNY *shakes his head. A pause.*

MICK *with controlled venom* : Yes, I have.

Shot 483.

Close-up of ROWNTREE, *with* BARNES *and* FORTINBRAS *behind him in soft focus, only a slight tensing of muscles shows the anger with which he hears* MICK's *words.*

MICK *off* : The thing I hate about you, Rowntree, is the way you give coca-cola to your scum, and your best teddy-bear to Oxfam . . .

Shot 484.

Big close-up of MICK. *He speaks with studied insolence.*

MICK : . . . and expect us to lick your frigid fingers for the rest of your frigid life.

Shot 485.

Big close-up of ROWNTREE, *very tense. Another pause.*

ROWNTREE *icy* : Go down to the gym. Wait outside.

Shot 486.

The empty corridor. MICK, JOHNNY *and* WALLACE *come into frame, walking fast down the corridor into long shot. They do not speak;* WALLACE *runs a little to catch up with the others.*

Shot 487.

Medium shot of MICK, JOHNNY *and* WALLACE *as they come into the lobby outside the gym, camera panning right with them. Gym clothes hang from pegs above benches against the walls right and left; double doors with frosted glass panes are opposite the camera, leading into the gym. The* Boys *line up casually on the right of frame:* Johnny *leans against the wall beside the doors, facing camera. We can hear footsteps as the* Whips *approach. They come into shot, passing* Mick, Johnny *and* Wallace *without looking at them, and go into the gym, closing the door behind them. There is a pause.*

Denson *off* : Wallace!

Wallace *takes off his jacket and hands it to* Mick, *who hangs it on a hook. Then he goes through the door into the gym. The other two stand motionless, listening. We hear footsteps running along the boards of the gym, then the crack of the cane. The steps return slowly, there is a slight pause, then the running begins again, and again the crack. It happens four times.* Mick *crosses and peers through the crack between the doors.* Johnny's *face shows nothing. Three. Four. Then* Rowntree's *voice.*

Rowntree *off* : Get up!

Mick *and* Johnny *exchange glances. Not too bad. Footsteps approach the gym door and* Wallace *comes through and joins the others. He is grinning.*

Wallace : Only four . . .

Mick *ruffles* Wallace's *hair as he passes.*

Denson *off* : Knightly!

Wallace *is about to move towards the bench by the wall, then stops.* Johnny *takes off his jacket and hands it to* Mick, *then goes into the gym.* Wallace *jumps up and down: he throws a few punches in the air. From inside the gym the sound of footsteps is followed by the sound of the cane.* Mick *peers through the crack between the doors. He looks back to* Wallace.

Mick : Christ, that was a bit low!

Wallace *has stopped jumping about: he undoes his trousers and turns, pulling his pants down trying to see the marks. The footsteps and the blows of the cane continue on the other side of the doors.*

Wallace : Hey Mick . . .

MICK *comes over and bends down to inspect.*
WALLACE : Blood?
MICK : Yeah . . . blood.

WALLACE *carefully pulls up his trousers, pleased.* MICK *straightens up and moves towards camera: only his restlessness and clasped hands show his tension. The footsteps and the fourth cane stroke are heard, then more footsteps and* JOHNNY *comes through the doors, closing them behind him.* MICK *makes immediately for the doors.*

DENSON *off* : Travis!
Simultaneously MICK *flings both doors open.*
Shot 488.
Medium close-up of MICK *standing in the doorway. He lets the doors close behind him and smiles, impertinently nonchalant.*
Shot 489.
Long shot of MICK *and the four* WHIPS *confronting each other. There is a pause, then* MICK *walks forward and faces* ROWNTREE.

ROWNTREE : Take off your coat. MICK *takes off his coat deliberately, holding it with one hand.* Go to the bars.

MICK *walks slowly and deliberately down to the bars, and drapes his jacket over one end. He turns to face the* WHIPS *at the far end of the gym, leaning indolently against the bar.*

ROWNTREE : Bend over.

MICK *turns back to face the bar, runs his hands out delicately on either side, proceeding all the time with a sort of whimsical indulgence; then he bends over. (Still on page 101)* ROWNTREE *looks at the other* WHIPS. *Then he looks back at* MICK. *He runs forward, giving him a tremendous swipe with his cane. He returns to his place, walking, pauses, then runs back and beats* MICK *again. He turns and walks back to the others.*
Shot 490.
Cut to the Sweat Room. Medium close-up of JUTE, *busying himself with a paper puzzle. Behind him another* BOY *at the desk against the wall; left of frame,* BILES.

119

They are sitting silently, listening. Camera tracks slowly left along the line of cubicles. ROWNTREE'S *footsteps can be heard, and the sound of the third cane stroke is like a distant gunshot.* BILES *shakes his head: he does not know why they are being beaten. He looks up anxiously. Next to him another small* BOY *leans his head against the side of the desk, listening. The track ends on a medium close-up of* BOBBY PHILLIPS, *also anxious. Behind him are* MARKLAND *and* BRUNNING. *Fourth stroke.*
Shot 491.
Close-up of MICK *bent almost double over the bar. He straightens up, camera panning with him, and reaches over for his coat. The four* WHIPS *are grouped together in the background, in soft focus.*
ROWNTREE *sharply* : Wait till you're told! Get down!
MICK *turns slowly and drops his coat back on to the bar. His eyes show his resentment, but he takes a deep breath and bends down again, camera panning down with him.*
Shot 492.
Medium close-up of WALLACE *and* JOHNNY *waiting outside the gym.* WALLACE *peers through the crack in the door. They look at each other, puzzled, as they hear* ROWNTREE *running down for a fifth stroke.*
Shot 493.
Close-up of MICK *bending over the bar.* ROWNTREE *runs in behind him and canes him again.* MICK *winces with pain and bites his lip.* ROWNTREE *walks back up the gym.*
Shot 494.
Medium close-up of STEPHANS *in his study, sucking a barleysugar stick. Photographs of Mrs. Wilson and Princess Anne in jodphurs are visible on the wall behind him. He listens with satisfaction as the footsteps and sixth stroke pierce the silence.*
Shot 495.
Close-up of MICK. *He has sunk lower, but still grips the bar, his knuckles white.* ROWNTREE *runs into shot and delivers another powerful stroke.* MICK *tenses with pain, but still controls himself.*

120

Shot 496.

Close-up of PEANUTS. *He listens, impassive, to the foot-steps in the distance, then turns slowly back to his microscope and looks into it.*

Shot 497.

Close-up of the slide under the microscope. Organisms divide and multiply in the pale green liquid, as footsteps and stroke ring out again.

Shot 498.

Long shot of ROWNTREE *in the gym.* DENSON, BARNES *and* FORTINBRAS *are looking at him.* FORTINBRAS *is beginning to look worried.* ROWNTREE *runs forward, passing camera in medium close-up, raising the cane in preparation. (Still on page 101) We hear the sound of the stroke out of shot.* ROWNTREE *walks back up the gym, and joins the other* WHIPS. *He is breathing heavily.*

ROWNTREE : Get up !

Shot 499.

Medium shot of MICK, *seen from behind, bent over the bar. There is a pause. Then slowly he forces himself erect, back to camera. He raises one hand stealthily to wipe away a tear. There is another pause. He turns towards camera, picking up his coat as he does so. His face is wet with tears, his expression defiant.*

Shot 500.

Long shot of the WHIPS. MICK *comes into shot and walks towards* ROWNTREE. *Pain, and the effort to disguise it, makes him walk slowly. He stops as* ROWNTREE *rests the cane on the floor, and holds out his hand. He takes* ROWNTREE'S *outstretched hand. (Still on page 102)*

MICK *just audibly* : Thank you, Rowntree.

ROWNTREE : Thank you.

MICK *walks painfully towards the door, camera panning with him. The* WHIPS *turn and watch him go. He opens the door, goes through and closes it behind him. Fade out.*

6

Shot 501. TITLE : RESISTANCE
  Fade out.
  Shot 502.
  Fade in on a long shot of the College and Chapel from outside. The organ accompanies treble voices singing the College song, the words are indistinct.
  Shot 503.
  Close-up of exterior Gothic window. The College song mixes into the sound of a voice reading Greek.
  Shot 504.
  The Library: an atmosphere of studious calm and shafted sunlight. Medium close-up of FORTINBRAS, *he is reading in Greek from Plato's* Republic.
FORTINBRAS : '. . . hosper tous skulakas . . .'
  The music fades out completely. Camera tracks slowly in and tilts up.
CLASSICS MASTER *off* : Thank you, Fortinbras.
  The tilt reveals the CLASSICS MASTER, *standing in front of the Classical Sixth, smoking a pipe. He wears dark glasses throughout the scene.*
CLASSICS MASTER : Translate, please.
  As FORTINBRAS *translates the passage, the* CLASSICS MASTER *strolls across in front of the window. A bust of Demosthenes is on the table behind him.*
FORTINBRAS : ' And do you not remember, I said, that we also said that we must conduct the children to war on horseback to . . . to be spectators . . .'
  Shot 505.
  Reverse angle featuring FORTINBRAS *and other* BOYS *in the class, following in their texts.*
FORTINBRAS : '. . . and wherever it may be safe, bring them to the front and give them a taste of blood . . . as we do with . . .' er . . .
  Shot 506.
  Medium close-up of CLASSICS MASTER, *waiting.*

FORTINBRAS *off*: '. . . *tous skulakas* . . .' er '. . . as we do with horses?'

The CLASSICS MASTER *paces meditatively, puffing on his pipe, camera panning with him. He turns affably.*

CLASSICS MASTER: A creditable guess . . . but no . . . Anyone else?

Shot 507.

Medium close-up of JACKSON *with* FORTINBRAS *and others in the background.*

JACKSON: A young she-goat?

Shot 508.

Medium close-up of the CLASSICS MASTER, *benign.*

CLASSICS MASTER: Look it up, Rowntree . . .

Shot 509.

Close-up of a large Greek lexicon. ROWNTREE'S *hands flip over several pages, and then pause.*

ROWNTREE *off*: 'Skulax . . . skulakas . . .' *Camera pans up to show* ROWNTREE *reading* '. . . a young dog . . . a whelp . . . a puppy.' *He looks up. The crack of an air-pistol.*

Shot 510.

Close-up of MICK *in his study. He is sitting on his couch, his back to the wall, aiming an air-pistol, a cigarette in his mouth. He lowers the pistol. Music begins.*

Shot 511.

Medium shot of MICK. *He stretches to the table beside him and selects a red dart. He re-loads, and takes the cigarette from his mouth, putting it down on the table. Carefully he takes aim.*

Shot 512.

A section of the collage on MICK'S *wall. A Paris Match double-spread of armed gendarmes drawn up in line holding round metal shields. Rising from the midst of them, a voluptuous nude. A sharp crack as* MICK'S *dart scores a bull's-eye on her right breast.*

Shot 513.

MICK *reloads, puts his cigarette back in his mouth, and takes aim.*

Shot 514.

A heavy, middle-aged bureaucrat or industrialist (prob-

ably French). A hand holding a packet of cigarettes lies over the neck of a golden retriever. MICK'S *dart gets Man's Best Friend on the muzzle.*
Shot 515.
MICK *takes aim again.*
Shot 516.
Audrey Hepburn and Mel Ferrer smile radiantly. General de Gaulle peers round the corner of the picture. A crack and Audrey Hepburn is hit right on the nose. There is a pause, then another crack, and another dart hits Mel Ferrer in the teeth.
Shot 517.
A happy bourgeois family—father, mother and son—snug in bed under an orange blanket. A Paris Guarde Militaire swoops in to the attack, baton upraised. MICK'S *blue dart hits the father in the midriff.*
Shot 518.
Medium shot of MICK. *He puts down his cigarette, and takes aim again.*
Shot 519.
A priest on the left of the collage: in the centre, a nude, her arms round a large tumescent missile. A red dart hits her on the bottom.
Shot 520.
An Arab fighter or refugee, his arms outspread in surrender: behind him, to left and right, some impotent international tribunal. MICK'S *dart lands in the refugee's chest.*
Shot 521.
An English aristocrat on his lawn; a Country Life *beauty; between them Big Ben. A dart cracks into the clock-face.*
Shot 522.
A wounded Vietnamese; a starving baby; two aperitif glasses. A dart lands in the centre of one of the glasses, then another in the second.
Shot 523.
Medium close-up of MICK. *He reloads and aims again, with special deliberation.*

Shot 524.
The Royal Coach. Bowler-hatted business types march
before it. The Queen waves, coronetted and smiling.
Shot 525.
Jump in closer as a red dart cracks into a bowler-hatted
gent seen through the front window of the carriage.
ROWNTREE *off* : For the first time in thirteen years . . .
Shot 526.
Medium long shot of ROWNTREE *standing behind the*
top table in the dining hall. DENSON, BARNES *and*
FORTINBRAS *stand in front of him, seen over the heads*
of BOYS *standing at their tables in the foreground.*
ROWNTREE : . . . College House has won the Bigley Memorial
Marathon Chalice. *Loud cheers.* ROWNTREE *raises his hand*
for quiet, his voice thick with emotion. This House has seen
great days . . . it's going to see them again. We're back on
the right track at last . . .
Shot 527.
Close-up of JUTE, *coming into shot carrying the chalice*
—a large silver challenge cup. Camera pans with him as
he passes the Junior table going into medium shot, to
hand the chalice to DENSON *and* BARNES.
ROWNTREE *off* : But I don't want you to think you can relax
It's up to everyone to pull together.
The pan reveals all the WHIPS. JUTE *returns and sits*
down at his place on the Junior table.
ROWNTREE : I want to see each one of you going all out. I
know you've got it in you. So let's see College House back
on top. *To* BARNES *and* DENSON : All right . . . *They hand*
him the chalice and he lifts it, holding it out. Right . . . House
Thump!
Led by the other three WHIPS, *who cheer and beat time*
with their canes, the BOYS *immediately start to yell and*
bang their fists or elbows on the table. The table is laid
for dinner and the rattle of crockery and cutlery adds
to the noise.
ALL *shouting* : College House! College House! College
House! College House! College House!
Camera pans down to the Juniors' table, where the

younger Boys *are banging and yelling almost hysterically.*
Shot 528.
Close-up of the collage in Mick's *study. The cheering
and banging is heard off, fading out as the camera pans
down to medium close-up of* Mick *tilting the vodka
bottle up to drain the last few drops. He takes a deep
breath, and sits forward, camera panning with him, as
he holds the bottle out to* Wallace, *who is squatting
on the floor in front of him.* Mick *pours a few drops into*
Wallace's *mouth then brings it across to* Johnny, *who
is squatting next to* Wallace. *The camera pans with
him until only his arm is in shot. The last few drops
trickle into* Johnny's *open mouth.*
Shot 529.
Close-up of Mick. *He looks at the bottle, turns it upside
down, and regretfully throws it away on to the couch.
He looks at* Johnny *and* Wallace.
Mick : We're on our own now . . .
Shot 530.
Close-up of Johnny *looking at him expectantly.*
Shot 531.
Close-up of Wallace.
Wallace : What are we going to do?
Shot 532.
Close-up of Mick. *He looks at them searchingly.*
Mick : Trust me?
Shot 533.
Close-up of Johnny.
Johnny : Of course.
Shot 534.
Close-up of Wallace.
Wallace : When are we going to do it?
Shot 535.
Close-up of Mick.
Mick : When I say.
He moves forward, going out of shot.
Shot 536.
Medium shot of Johnny *and* Wallace, *watching*
Mick *closely. He leans over to a drawer in his desk, left*

of screen, and takes out his cut-throat razor. Music begins. MICK *kneels back in front of* JOHNNY *and* WALLACE, *opens the razor and draws it carefully across his open right hand, at the base of his thumb. He shows them his palm, blood beginning to seep from the cut. Silently* JOHNNY *and* WALLACE *hold out their hands.* MICK *makes a similar cut in each. They look at their hands.* MICK *clasps* JOHNNY'S *hand to his, palm to palm.*

MICK *solemnly* : Death to the oppressor! *(Still on page 102)*

JOHNNY *clasps* WALLACE'S *hand.*

JOHNNY : The Resistance!

WALLACE *clasps* MICK'S *hand.*

WALLACE : Liberty!

Shot 537.

Close-up of MICK.

MICK : One man can change the world—with a bullet in the right place.

He gets up suddenly and moves across towards the window, out of shot. Camera focuses back on the collage-covered wall: Lenin in his Polish cap.

Shot 538.

Medium close-up of MICK, *back to camera, leaning out of the window. He is feeling for something with his right hand. He turns back to the others, and camera pans down, passing* WALLACE *and bringing* JOHNNY *into shot.*

MICK : Real bullets . . .

The camera pans down on their outstretched hands. MICK'S *hand puts two bullets into each of their palms. He holds his own hand out beside theirs—three bullets lying in his bloodstained palm. Recorder music can be heard off, with singing.*

MR. KEMP *singing, off* : ' Fairest . . .'

Shot 539.

Cut to the KEMPS' *bedroom: pink floral paper; two brass bedsteads; between them a gilt-framed portrait of a gowned academic. In medium shot,* MR. KEMP *is sitting on the edge of his bed, in pyjamas.* MRS. KEMP *is sitting up in her bed, accompanying him rather*

131

uncertainly on the recorder. (Still on page 103)

MR. KEMP *singing :* '. . . isle, all isles excelling,
Seat of pleasure and of love,
Venus here shall choose her dwelling . . .'

Shot 540.

Cut to MATRON'S *room. She is sitting in a rocking chair, dozing in front of the fire. Camera tracks in slowly to hold her in a dreaming close-up. The tune is taken up by a musical box.*

MR. KEMP *singing, off :* '. . . And forsake her Cyprian grove.'
MATRON *strokes the cushion behind her head; her mouth twitches in a sensual smile. The Purcell theme fades into atmospheric orchestral chords.*

*Shot 541. (Black and white stock, sepia tint.)

Dissolve to the Junior Dormitory. It is dark. BOYS *are asleep in their beds. Camera pans slowly along the line —*MARKLAND, MACHIN, *ending on a high angle close-up of a bed in which* BOBBY PHILLIPS *is lying,* WALLACE'S *arm around him, very peaceful. (Still on page 103)*

*Shot 542.

Shot of the night sky through a telescope.

*Shot 543.

High angle medium shot from the outside, of a House window. Inside we see PEANUTS, *looking out through a telescope.* MICK *walks into shot and stands in the gloom looking out.* PEANUTS *glances up at him, then back at the night sky.*

PEANUTS : Space, you see Michael, is all expanding—at the speed of light.

*Shot 544.

Shot of the night sky, clear and full of stars.

PEANUTS *off :* It's a mathematical certainty that somewhere among all those millions of stars, there's . . .

*Shot 545.

Medium shot of the two BOYS *at the window.*

PEANUTS : . . . another planet where they speak English.
PEANUTS *moves up to the window.* MICK *looks thoughtfully at the bullets in his hand and then hands one to* PEANUTS. PEANUTS *looks at it, then returns it to* MICK

132

without comment.
PEANUTS *indicating the telescope* : Have a look . . .
Shot 546.
Close-up of MICK *squinting through the telescope.*
Shot 547.
The night sky through the telescope. Camera pans down from the sky, past a chimney, down the side of the House till it reaches an open, lighted window, where the GIRL *from the café is brushing her hair. She looks up, smiles and waves a hand. Music stops. Fade out.*

7

Shot 548. Title :   FORTH TO WAR
   Fade out.
   Shot 549.
   Fade in on a side angle of the Chapel windows.
Chaplain *off* : 'The Son of God goes forth to war . . . a kingly crown to gain.'
   *Shot 550. (Black and white stock, magenta tint.)
   Medium shot of the Chaplain *in the pulpit. He leans forward.*
Chaplain : We are all corrupt. We are all sinful. We are all meet to be punished. If a soldier doesn't do his duty, he expects to be punished.
   *Shot 551.
   High angle long shot of the Boys *sitting listening in the Chapel. They are all wearing the College Cadet Corps uniform.*
Chaplain *off* : There are failures great and small, and there are punishments great and small. But . . . there is one failure, one crime . . .
   *Shot 552.
   Medium close-up of the Chaplain.
Chaplain : . . . one betrayal—that can never be forgiven— and that betrayal is called desertion. The deserter in the face of the enemy must expect to be shot.
   *Shot 553.
   High angle medium close-up of Jute *from behind, in his College Cadet Corps uniform, sitting among other Juniors in uniform. He looks back over his shoulder, up towards the pulpit.*
Chaplain *off* : Jesus Christ is our commanding officer, and if we desert him, we can expect no mercy !
   *Shot 554.
   Medium close-up of the Chaplain. *He leans forward again, hands clasped.*
Chaplain : And . . . we are all—deserters !

Shot 555.
Medium close-up of JUTE, seen from above, looking up wide-eyed. All the other BOYS are motionless, backs to camera. Drums crash in.
Shot 556. (Return to colour.)
Long shot across the grass, of the College buildings, cloisters, and the main Chapel door. Led by the CHAPLAIN in full military uniform, riding a chestnut horse, the College Cadet Corps marches out to the sound of bugles and drums. Three platoons, then the Corps band playing a rousing march, then an armoured car and another platoon. The bugles stop, but the drumming continues.
Shot 557. (Black and white stock, magenta tint.)
Cut to the empty corridor in College House.
Shot 558.
Close-up of a broken chair with initials and dates going back to the nineteenth century carved on the seat.
Shot 559.
Close-up of a jumble of games clothes and a hockey-stick, thrown together on the floor of the gym. Atmospheric orchestral music mixes in over the Corps band.
Shot 560.
Long shot of the dormitory corridor. MRS. KEMP wanders down the corridor towards camera. She is naked, and her hair hangs loose about her shoulders. The orchestral music fades out.
Shot 561. (Return to colour.)
The road running along the College field. Medium shot of the CHAPLAIN leading the parade. (Still on page 104) He rides out of shot, followed by the first platoon.
Shot 562.
Close-up of boots marching past camera.
Shot 563. (Black and white stock, magenta tint.)
Medium shot of MRS. KEMP, walking naked through the Senior Dormitory, away from camera. The drums and marching feet fade out and the music mixes back. She moves slowly as if in a dream, caressing a wash bowl, passing between the wash-stands and beds. (Still on page 104) She stops and fingers a bar of soap, then a towel.

135

Shot 564.

Close-up of MRS. KEMP. *She turns and looks over her shoulder. No one is there to see.*

Shot 565. (Return to colour.)

A wood: small trees with greenish trunks. The ground slopes from right to left. Rifle and machine-gun fire. A College House platoon is running, spread out, through the undergrowth. Camera tracks with the leaders— including PUSSY GRAVES—*till they come to a halt behind a fallen tree.* KEATING *has a large portable wireless set on his back.* MICK, JOHNNY *and* WALLACE *lurk in the background.* DENSON *is in command.*

DENSON : Now, Corporal ... here ...

STEPHENS *steps forward and stands next to him.* DENSON *points.*

DENSON : Now that's our objective, where that tree is. Right? DENSON *turns to address the rest of the troop.* Now listen, D. Section . . . Come on, listen. Hedge junction, four o'clock, bushy top tree. *He gestures towards the hedge and tree, which are out of shot.* We will attack and destroy that tree. Right —Bren gun left! *Nobody moves.* Go on, move!

STEPHANS *shoves* JOHNNY *forward.* WALLACE *and* MICK *follow him,* WALLACE *carrying the Bren gun. They clamber off out of shot. The others stand looking after them.*

Shot 566.

Long shot of MICK, JOHNNY *and* WALLACE *running out of the wood and along the line of a fence.* MR. THOMAS *runs into shot, gesturing. He blows on his referee's whistle and waves his arm (he has a red armband), signalling them to get the other side of the fence. They climb over and plough through dense undergrowth, tripping over the thick brambles.*

Shot 567.

Long shot of the CHAPLAIN *on his horse, scanning the horizon through binoculars. Some cadets run over the brown bracken in the background: indistinct orders are shouted. The whistle blows again.*

A VOICE *off* : Single file! Single file!

Shot 568.

Medium shot of MICK, JOHNNY *and* WALLACE *struggling through brambles and bracken on the other side of a fence, hampered by their packs and rifles. Behind them on the edge of a field of stubble more cadets run in single file in the opposite direction. Occasional shots ring out.* MICK *stumbles down into the ditch. He climbs through a gap in the fence and takes the Bren gun from* WALLACE *as he follows him.*

A VOICE : Well done, that man with the Bren![1]

Shot 569.

Medium shot of DENSON *and* STEPHANS *running towards camera and dropping down in to the bracken. Indistinct orders of* ' Rabbit crawl, man!' *mixed with machine gun fire. The other members of D. Section can be seen in the background.* DENSON *takes the field glasses from* STEPHANS *who beckons up the section. They run forward then drop down closer to* DENSON *and* STEPHANS. DENSON *looks round impatiently, then hands the glasses back to* STEPHANS, *who raises them to his eyes.*

Shot 570.

A bracken-covered slope. MICK, JOHNNY *and* WALLACE *scramble up out of a leafy ditch, into medium shot. They flop down wearily on some faded grass.*

BOY *off* : Aaaaaaaaaagh!

They look up in surprise.

Shot 571.

BOY *off* : Aaaaaaaaaaagh!

Medium long shot of a line of Junior BOYS, *including* JUTE, MACHIN, BILES *and* BRUNNING, *as they tear down a slope towards camera in a bayonet charge. They finish in medium shot.* PEANUTS *bounds into shot after them, shouting and waving his rifle.*

PEANUTS : Stop! *The younger* BOYS *turn back to him.* What are you doing? It's awful! You forgot to yell . . . the yell of hate!

He jabs forward suddenly, stabbing with his bayonet.

---

[1] End of reel four.

His mouth opens wide. (Still on page 121)
Shot 572.
Close-up of PEANUTS, *his wide-gapped teeth savage in his distended mouth, his eyes glinting behind his horn-rimmed glasses. He lets loose a blood-curdling yell.*

PEANUTS : Aaaaaaaaaaagh !
He straightens up, camera tilting with him. His face reverts to its normal expression of equanimity.

PEANUTS : It's the yell that counts. Everybody back. *He turns and hurries away up the slope again, out of shot. Off :* At the double! *The* JUNIOR BOYS *hurry after him.*
Shot 573.
Long shot of PEANUTS *and his* JUNIORS *running back to the top of the rise; they stop, turn towards camera, and line up with bayonets forward.*

PEANUTS : Ready? Charge!
The JUNIORS *charge down the hill towards camera, screaming horribly.*

BOYS : Aaaaaaaaaaaagh !
Shot 574.
The sound cuts off sharply. Medium long shot of WALLACE, MICK *and* JOHNNY *trudging towards camera in single file. A skylark sings piercingly above. Suddenly the peace is shattered by an explosion. They stop,* WALLACE *sinking to his knees, and look down curiously. Explosions and gunfire.*

VOICE *off :* Charge!
They look in the direction of the command. Shouting and yelling off.
Shot 575.
High angle general shot looking down across the red leaf-strewn ground to a clearing in the woods, with a group of black tin huts in a hollow. Smoke is pouring out of the nearest hut. From all sides, cadets run into shot and down towards the huts, yelling and firing. One mortar shell explodes, then another. Opposing Bren fire from the huts. More cadets run in and take cover, yelling Red Indian fashion; they kneel to fire and run on down. A few cadets fall. The attack reaches the huts.

138

Shot 576.
Again a sharp sound cut. Long shot of grass-covered hill.
MICK, JOHNNY *and* WALLACE *trail forward wearily towards camera. They stop suddenly as a whistle blows shrilly in front of them.*
MR. THOMAS *off* : Stop there!
Shot 577.
MR. THOMAS *has popped up in medium shot behind a gorse-bush.*
MR. THOMAS *excitedly* : Get down, get down, get down!
He lights a thunderflash and hurls it towards them.
Shot 578.
Medium long shot of MICK, JOHNNY *and* WALLACE, *vaguely puzzled. The thunderflash lands and explodes at* WALLACE'S *feet. Indulgently, they all sink to the ground.*
Shot 579.
Medium close-up of MR. THOMAS, *beaming with pleasure.*
MR. THOMAS : You're all dead . . . *triumphantly* . . . I've won!
Shot 580.
Medium close-up of the CHAPLAIN *on his horse, peering disapprovingly off screen; then he rides out right. The shouting continues, off.*
Shot 581.
Medium long shot of MICK, JOHNNY *and* WALLACE *sitting exhausted on the grass.*
VOICE *off* : Get into line! Come on, move!
The CHAPLAIN'S *horse trots past, arrogantly, in close shot. They look up and watch him go past, without moving.*
Shot 582.
Close-up of MICK. *He has a little sprig of gorse tucked into the badge on his beret. He takes his beret off and stares with hatred after the* CHAPLAIN. *The whistle blows again.*
CHAPLAIN *off* : All right . . .
Shot 583.
Very long shot of the Corps assembling in a clearing,

139

*where the lorries and the armoured car are parked. An
urn has been set up in the back of one of the lorries, and
everyone is drinking tea, moving around, queueing, and
eating little cakes. A platoon is marching in from right
of screen.*

CHAPLAIN : . . . Denson, bring your men over here. Hurry up !
Now, march, properly . . . hup, hup, hup ! That's right . . .
pick up your mugs.

    MR. THOMAS *supervises the tea queue.*

A VOICE : At the double . . .

    Shot 584.

    Medium close-up of JOHNNY *crouched behind a screen
of gorse; he brings his rifle forward cautiously.*

CHAPLAIN *off* : Come on boy, don't hang about . . .

    *A general buzz of chatter can be heard from the clearing,
off. Camera pans from* JOHNNY *to medium close-up of*
WALLACE, *behind his Bren gun, pointing over the top of
the brambles. He gets a view through his sights. The pan
continues past* WALLACE *to a close-up of* MICK *with his
rifle: he shoves the safety-catch forward, and takes aim.*

CHAPLAIN *off* : Who left these mugs here? . . . Right—hurry
up, hurry up, hurry up !

    Shot 585.

    Medium close-up of the CHAPLAIN *as he struts forward in
front of the* BOYS, *who are standing and sitting around,
drinking tea and eating buns.*

CHAPLAIN : D Section over here—this is an order !

    Camera pans back with the CHAPLAIN *as he goes to the
back of the lorry where* MR. THOMAS *is filling mugs of tea
for a queue of* BOYS. *Camera holds them in medium
close-up. At the head of the line,* JUTE *takes his mug of
tea.*

CHAPLAIN : All right, boy? JUTE *nods.* That's right . . . you
keep going.

    The CHAPLAIN *goes out of shot with an arm round* JUTE'S
shoulders. MR. THOMAS *continues to pour tea for the*
BOYS *waiting in line. He hands a mug of tea to* BILES.
*Suddenly rifle fire hits the tea-urn with a resounding clang
and a dangerous ricochet. Tea begins to pour out of the*

140

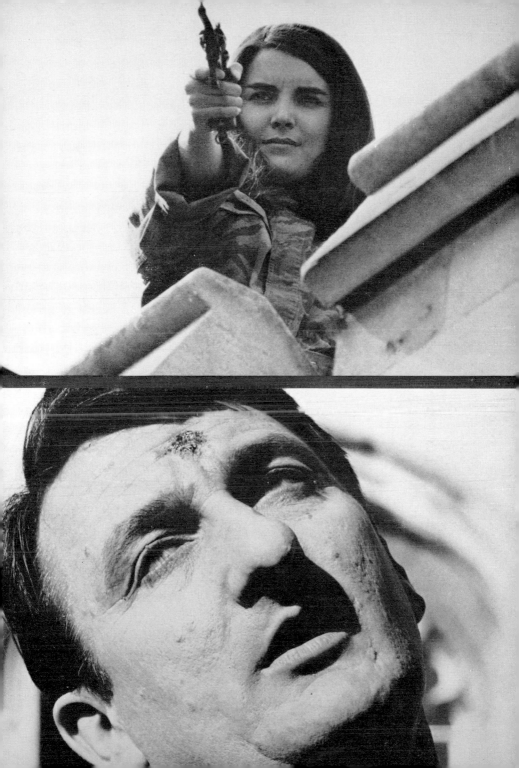

holes. MR. THOMAS *looks wildly round and flings himself to the ground.* BILES *stands and stares, stupefied. The air is filled with rifle and machine gun fire.*
Shot 586.
Long shot of the clearing. Cadets are flinging themselves to the ground or diving behind the lorries and trestle tables for cover. The CHAPLAIN *stands firm by the tea-urn.*
CHAPLAIN : Take cover! *(Still on page 121)*
Shot 587.
Close-up of the passenger window of the lorry as bullets smash through it.
Shot 588.
Medium close-up of PEANUTS *lying under the lorry, hands over his head.*
CHAPLAIN *off, shouting above the din* : Take cover!
Shot 589.
Medium shot of MR. THOMAS *lying on the ground—tea from the urn is pouring on to him. He looks round nervously.*
CHAPLAIN *off, shouting* : Who's there?
Shot 590.
Medium shot as someone pushes one of the trestle tables over; mugs and sausage rolls cascade to the ground. Camera pans down with it. The firing ceases abruptly. No one moves or speaks.
Shot 591.
Long shot of the CHAPLAIN, *the only man still on his feet. He is surrounded by prostrate cadets.*
CHAPLAIN *shouting* : Who's there? Show yourself, whoever you are! *He marches forward briskly and stops in medium close-up.* Come out of there!
Shot 592.
Long shot of trees and gorse bushes, across an expanse of heath beyond the field. MICK, JOHNNY *and* WALLACE *stand up and step forward.* JOHNNY *and* WALLACE *relax;* MICK *holds his rifle at the ready.*
Shot 593.
Close-up of the CHAPLAIN, *coming towards them.*
CHAPLAIN *shouting* : Empty those rifles at once! Hand over

145

those rifles instantly. *He walks forward out of shot.*
   Shot 594.
   Long shot of the three Boys. *They have stopped and are standing in a line. The* Chaplain *walks commandingly towards them, back to camera.*
Chaplain : Come on, hand them over !
   As the Chaplain *approaches,* Mick *raises his rifle to aim. (Still on page 122) The* Chaplain *checks slightly, then continues to walk with the confidence of authority. He is mistaken.* Mick *fires. The* Chaplain *lurches, then falls heavily on his side.*
   Shot 595.
   High angle medium shot of the Chaplain, *lying on the ground. He raises a hand.*
Chaplain : For the love of God ! *Desperately* : Don't shoot ! Don't shoot !
   Shot 596.
   Low angle medium shot as Mick *moves steadily forward, bayonet fixed. He fires, then continues to move forward until he is in medium close-up. He raises his rifle, bayonet threatening the object on the ground at his feet. An instant's pause.*
   Shot 597.
   High angle shot of the Chaplain *writhing on the ground, whimpering in terrified anticipation of the cold steel.*
   Shot 598.
   Low angle close-up of Mick, *with bayonet poised. His mouth opens in the yell of Hate.*
Mick : Aaaaaaaaagh ! *He thrusts forward and down, out of shot. Camera holds on the open sky as the long savage cry rings out.*
   Shot 599.
   Cut to the Headmaster's *study: panelling, framed groups and portraits. Medium close-up of the window, luminous behind white net curtains. The* Headmaster *comes into shot, pacing past the window, his face set and serious. The camera pans till he stops behind his desk, and looks off with a self-consciously grave expression.*

146

HEADMASTER: I take this very seriously . . . very seriously indeed.

Shot 600.

Medium shot of MICK, JOHNNY *and* WALLACE *standing in a row. The* HEADMASTER *stands opposite them in the foreground. Their faces are expressionless.*

HEADMASTER: The Reverend Woods might have been quite badly hurt. Do you realise that?

Shot 601.

Medium shot as the HEADMASTER *walks slowly away from his desk over to a huge cupboard, the bottom half lined with deep drawers.*

HEADMASTER: Now I want you to apologise to him. Is that clear?

Shot 602.

Medium close-up of JOHNNY, MICK *and* WALLACE *standing silently, impassive.*

Shot 603.

In medium shot, the HEADMASTER *heaves the first drawer of the cupboard open. The* CHAPLAIN *sits up in it, now in his gown and dog-collar, (Still on page 122) and stretches out a hand with Christian charity.* MICK, WALLACE *and* JOHNNY *file past in silence, shake his hand and file back. The* HEADMASTER *nods dismissively and the* CHAPLAIN *lies back. The* HEADMASTER *pushes the drawer closed again behind him, and speaks with immense, insidious blandness.*

HEADMASTER: Now you mustn't think that I don't understand. *He moves forward, camera panning back with him, past* WALLACE *in back view in the foreground.* It's a natural characteristic of adolescence to want to proclaim individuality. *Camera pans and tracks sideways, passing behind* JOHNNY *and* MICK *as the* HEADMASTER *crosses in front of them.* There's nothing unhealthy about that. It's a quite blameless form of existentialism. *The* HEADMASTER *sinks back into a small armchair in front of the boys, informal yet still authoritative.* MICK *is visible in the foreground, back to camera.* This, for instance, is what lies at the heart of the great Hair Problem. *He crosses his left leg over his right with elegant, demonstrative relaxation*. I think you boys know that I keep an open mind on most things.

Shot 604.

Close-up of WALLACE. *Camera pans slowly along to a close-up of* MICK. *They might be looking at a man from the Moon.*

HEADMASTER *off* : And of one thing I am certain : short hair is no indication of merit. So often I have noticed that it's the hair rebels who step into the breach when there's a crisis— whether it be a fire in the House, or to sacrifice a week's holiday in order to give a party of slum children seven days in the country.

Shot 605.

Close-up of the HEADMASTER.

HEADMASTER : But, of course, there are limits. Scruffiness of any kind is deplorable. *He stands up, camera tilting up with him.* I think you'd go that far with me? *He stares at them searchingly, then turns to walk to the window.*

Shot 606.

Close-up of MICK *and* JOHNNY. JOHNNY *glances sideways at* MICK, *but* MICK'S *eyes do not swerve from the* HEAD-MASTER.

HEADMASTER *off* : Now the fees here are . . .

Shot 607.

Medium close-up from behind of the HEADMASTER *standing by the window and looking out, a classical bust on the table beside him.*

HEADMASTER : . . . at present six hundred and forty-three pounds per annum, which works out at about fifteen guineas a week. *He turns back to the* BOYS. This is no mean sum. It is the salary, for instance, of the average trainee supermarket manager. But, on the other hand, it's no more than the cost of keeping a juvenile delinquent in Borstal. However, this is merely to look at the matter . . .

Shot 608.

Medium close-up of MICK, JOHNNY *and* WALLACE *looking at the* HEADMASTER.

HEADMASTER *continuing, off* : . . . in terms of hard cash, which is not the only consideration . . .

148

Shot 609.

Back to the HEADMASTER *as he returns to stand behind his desk. The* BOYS *are in the foreground, backs to camera.*

HEADMASTER : There is, above all, the question of Service. Those who are given most also have most to give.

Shot 610.

Medium close-up of MICK, JOHNNY *and* WALLACE, *impassive to the end.*

HEADMASTER *off* : Now, you boys are intelligent. You're too intelligent to be rebels. That's too easy.

Shot 611.

Medium long shot of the HEADMASTER *over the heads of the* BOYS *in the foreground.*

HEADMASTER : And it would be easy to punish you in the normal way. But I'm going to give you a privilege : work. Real work. And I want you to think of this not as a punishment, but as an opportunity to give . . . to Serve.

Shot 612.

Long shot of the school Hall, from the stage. Panelling, portraits, Gothic windows. Silver cups in a glass case at the end of the Hall. Hundreds of chairs are stacked up in the main part of the Hall. The stage is littered with junk. BOBBY PHILLIPS *sits on the edge of it, leafing through a book. He turns and looks as a trap-door is suddenly thrown back and* JOHNNY *climbs out in medium shot, wearing a gas-mask and carrying a plaster bust. He chucks the bust to the ground and takes off the gas-mask.* WALLACE *hurries into shot, and they both bend down over the trap-door to heave something up.*

Shot 613.

Reverse shot of the stage from the Hall. Beyond JOHNNY *and* WALLACE *is a large stained-glass window, under it the College War Memorial. With much effort the* BOYS *pull a huge stuffed alligator out of the trap-door. They manhandle it to the horizontal.* PHILLIPS *comes over and takes the tail end from* JOHNNY. *Camera pans slightly with* WALLACE *and* PHILLIPS *as they carry it off the stage.* JOHNNY *lets go.*

149

Shot 614.

In medium shot, JOHNNY *turns and climbs back down through the trap-door, while* WALLACE *and* BOBBY *carry the alligator down the steps, through the Hall.*
Shot 615.

The yard outside the Hall. Medium shot of WALLACE *and* PHILLIPS *carrying the alligator under an arch. Camera pans with them to a huge bonfire blazing near the outside wall. A* MASTER *stands on duty and watches as the* BOYS *tip the alligator on to the blaze. They go back into the Hall; the* MASTER *stays by the fire, leaning against the wall, as flames envelope the alligator. Music.*
*Shot 616. (Black and white stock, magenta tint.)

A cluttered storage space under the stage. Close-up of a pile of assorted junk at the foot of the ladder up to the trap-door. Books, stuffed animals, old papers parcelled up. A stuffed monkey lands on the pile; then an armful of old books; then some old flags. Camera tilts up as JOHNNY *throws down these last. We see* MICK *in the background, clambering about among old desks. A map of the British Empire is upside down against the wall: stacks of old name-boards and discarded school parapher-nalia. Camera pans left with* JOHNNY *as he crosses in medium close-up and takes an armful of books down from a shelf. Camera pans back with him as he dumps them on the pile.* MICK *comes forward holding a stuffed eagle. He hands it to* JOHNNY. JOHNNY *looks at it, grinning, then puts it down on an old desk next to him. He strokes its head.* MICK *moves into the background again, and camera pans with* JOHNNY *in medium close-up as he moves right, then stops, his attention caught by some-thing. Then camera tracks as he walks forward to a cupboard. He throws down a blackboard and easel and some dusty old picture frames that are leaning against the cupboard door. The music stops,* JOHNNY *tries to open it, but it is padlocked. He looks back over his shoulder to* MICK.
*Shot 617.

Medium shot of MICK, *standing at the foot of the ladder,*

150

holding a plaster bust. He looks up at JOHNNY *and chucks the bust away. He picks up an axe, and camera tracks with him as he crosses to* JOHNNY, *standing in medium close-up in front of the cupboard.* MICK *gives the padlock a blow with his axe. It is so rotten that the catch breaks immediately. He puts the axe down and pulls the double doors open. Music starts again.* MICK *and* JOHNNY *stand and look: the cupboard shelves are lined with glass bottles and jars.*
*Shot 618.
Close-up of MICK, *with* JOHNNY *just behind him. They both catch sight of something particularly strange on the top shelf. (Still on page 123)*
*Shot 619.
Close-up of the rows of jars on the top shelf. They are old biological specimens preserved in spirit: in the centre, in a glass jar, a human foetus. (Still on page 123)
MICK'S *hands come into shot and lift it down. Camera pulls back slightly and pans slowly as* MICK *holds the bottle close, examining the never-born child. (Still on page 123) He turns towards* JOHNNY, *holding the jar between them. Camera tilts down as he lowers it to waist level. The hands of the* GIRL *from the café come into shot, enfolding the jar. (Still on page 123) She takes it from* MICK. *Camera tilts up to a shot of the* GIRL: *she looks at* MICK *and* JOHNNY. *(Still on page 123) Without a word she goes between them to the cupboard, camera panning with her. Camera pans with her hands only as she replaces the bottle on the shelf, (Still on page 123) and firmly closes the cupboard doors. The music comes to an end.*
*Shot 620.
Low angle medium shot of WALLACE *as he climbs down to the foot of the ladder, glancing back up to where* PHILLIPS *is climbing down after him. Camera pans with* WALLACE *as he joins* MICK, JOHNNY *and the* GIRL *by the cupboard.* MICK *climbs up on the desks beside the cupboard, and through the gap between it and the wall, followed by the* GIRL *and* JOHNNY. WALLACE *looks back*

151

over his shoulder, then he follows the others.[1]
*Shot 621.

Medium long shot as MICK *climbs through, emerging on the other side of the cupboard. It is very dark, with only a little light seeping through the cracks in the floorboards above.* MICK *helps the* GIRL *as she clambers down, and* JOHNNY *follows her.* MICK *lights a match. The* GIRL *finds a light switch and turns it on. They stand and look.*
*Shot 622.

Long shot from MICK'S *and the* GIRL'S *point of view. Camera pans down from the bare light bulb to show crates of ammunition and guns stacked up on top of each other all round the cellar. The* GIRL, MICK *and* JOHNNY *move forward, into shot.* MICK *grabs a bayonet and starts to lever open one of the ammunition boxes.* WALLACE *and* PHILLIPS *join them.*
*Shot 623.

Music begins. Medium close-up of MICK. *He looks up from the open box, a strange expression of mingled awe and excitement on his face.*
*Shot 624.

Close-up of MICK'S *hands, from above. They carefully lift a mortar shell out of the crate. Camera tilts up as he raises it.*
*Shot 625.

Medium close-up of the GIRL, *her eyes shining.*
*Shot 626.

Medium close-up of JOHNNY. *He kneels, staring, and camera pans slightly back in* MICK'S *direction.*
*Shot 627.

Low angle medium close-up of MICK. *He hands the shell to* JOHNNY, *who is out of shot.*
*Shot 628.

Medium close-up of the GIRL. *She has found another ammunition case and she prises it open. Camera tilts down to show the case, full of hand grenades.*
*Shot 629.

Medium shot of MICK : *he is distributing mortar shells.*

[1] End of reel five.

152

He turns and hands one to WALLACE *behind him, who has got hold of a mortar tube. He hands another down to* BOBBY PHILLIPS, *out of frame.*
*Shot 630.
Medium close-up from above of* PHILLIPS *kneeling beside another crate. He takes the mortar shell from* MICK.
*Shot 631.
Medium shot of* JOHNNY *picking up cartons of bullets. Camera pans over to the* GIRL *who has found another case full of shells.*
*Shot 632.
Long shot of all four* BOYS *and the* GIRL *as they break open cases, and hand ammunition, bombs and grenades to each other. The music fades out with the frame.*

8

Shot 633. Title :   CRUSADERS

Denson *off* : Guard of honour . . . 'shun!

> *Fade out title.*
> *Shot 634.*
> *Fade in on a low angle medium shot of the Union Jack flying in the wind. The Chapel clock chimes. Camera zooms out to long shot of the flag flying from the top of the College tower. Roofs and battlements can be seen.*

Denson *off* : Guard! Shoulder . . . arms!

> *Motorcycle engines roar in.*
> *Shot 635.*
> *Long shot of the College courtyard: grass and grey stone.* General Denson's *car, in camouflage green, drives in from the road, escorted by two military policemen on motorcycles.*

Denson *off* : Guard! Pre-sent . . . arms!

> *Camera pans with the car as it passes* Denson *and a small troop of cadets who present arms smartly. The car swings round to approach camera, stopping with the two outriders in medium shot.*

Denson : Guard! Shoulder arms!

> Denson *marches over to greet* General Denson, *who emerges from the car. He is in uniform. The two motor cycles and the car drive past camera and on out of shot.* Denson *and* General Denson *cross back to the guard and start a brisk inspection.*
> *Shot 636.*
> *Medium shot of* Biles *carrying the processional crucifix, with* Jute *and* Machin *behind him. They are all wearing surplices, their hair neatly smoothed down. A man in full armour with a scarlet cloak stands behind them.*

Denson *off* : Guard! Order . . . arms!

> General Denson *comes into medium shot, camera panning with him as* Rowntree *comes forward to greet him. They exchange greetings. The pan continues as he*

passes the choristers and two further red-cloaked KNIGHTS
in armour. The BISHOP, *in full robes, cope and mitre and
shepherd's crook comes to greet the* GENERAL *like an old
friend—which he is. They shake hands warmly and
exchange greetings. (Still on page 124)* DENSON *marches
through in the foreground, and* BILES, JUTE *and* MACHIN
follow him in the background with the crucifix. ROWN-
TREE *walks over and escorts the* GENERAL *and the*
BISHOP *away into the Hall. An organ introduction begins.*

VOICES *singing, off*: ' Stand up! Stand up, for College . . .'
Shot 637.
*Long shot of the College Hall, from the stage. The Hall
is crowded with visitors,* PARENTS *and some* BOYS. *The
men are in suits and uniforms, the women in their elegant
speech-day best, most with yellow or red summery hats.
They are all standing, singing the College song.* BILES,
JUTE *and* MACHIN *slowly lead the procession down the
aisle.*

VOICES *singing*: ' Each manly voice up-raise!
Clasp each the hand in brotherhood,
And raise the roof with praise! '
Shot 638.
*Reverse long shot, looking towards the stage on which
the* HEADMASTER *stands waiting, also singing, his* STAFF
*ranged in chairs behind him. Two empty chairs await
the* GENERAL *and the* BISHOP. *The procession moves
slowly forward, behind* BILES' *cross.*

VOICES *singing*: ' And when these days of school are past,
Though near we be or far . . .'
Shot 639.
Side angle medium long shot of BILES *and the other
two* JUNIORS *leading the procession between the rows
of spectators. The* BISHOP *follows, then* DENSON, *the*
GENERAL, *with* ROWNTREE *and the three* KNIGHTS *in
armour. Camera pans as* BILES, JUTE, MACHIN *and the*
BISHOP *walk on out of shot, and holds on the* GENERAL,
who looks round at the well-remembered walls.

VOICES *singing*: ' We'll cherish still her memory,
'Gainst fire and flood and foe,

155

We'll serve her still through good and ill,
As through the world we'll go.'

Shot 640.

Long shot towards the stage. The JUNIORS *peel off to either side. The* BISHOP *climbs slowly up on to the stage, followed by* DENSON, *the* GENERAL *and the rest of the procession.*

ALTOS, TREBLES *and* LADIES *singing:*

' And when these days of school are past,
Though near we be or far . . .'

Shot 641.

Long shot from the back of the stage as the GENERAL *comes up the steps: the* HEADMASTER *signals him courteously to a chair. He is followed by the senior* KNIGHT, *who takes up a position opposite the* HEAD-MASTER *near the front of the stage.*

ALL *singing:* ' We'll stand again for College,
Who made us what we are.'

Shot 642.

Low angle long shot from the Hall of the HEAD-MASTER, *the* KNIGHT *and the other visitors and* STAFF *assembled on the stage. The College song ends, and the* HEADMASTER *steps forward to kneel in front of the* KNIGHT. *Ceremoniously he kisses his gauntleted hand. He rises and the* KNIGHT *speaks.*

KNIGHT: Quidque vult, O custos?

HEADMASTER: Maxime, Benefactores. *(Still on page 124) The* HEADMASTER *turns towards the audience.*

Shot 643.

High angle long shot of the audience standing up, seen past the people on the stage.

ALL : Gratias vobis agimus, Benefactores.

Everyone sits down again. Much coughing, shuffling of feet etc.

Shot 644.

High angle medium shot of MATRON *and* MRS. KEMP *as they sit.*

Shot 645.

High angle medium shot of KEATING *settling moodily*

into his seat beside his mother. Ladies adjust their furs.
Everyone is looking expectantly towards the stage.
Shot 646.
Medium long shot of the HEADMASTER *standing on the*
stage. After a suitable pause he speaks, in confident,
ringing tones.
HEADMASTER : Your Royal Highness, my Lord Bishop,
General Denson, my Lords, Ladies and Gentlemen : today
is a day for the future, and also a day for the past . . . Any
institution which has half a . . .
Shot 647.
Long shot of the Hall. BOYS, PARENTS *and flowered*
hats sit listening with polite attention. Silver cups gleam
in the glass case at the back.
HEADMASTER *off* : . . . thousand years—one quarter of the
Christian era—stretching behind it is bound to have a sense
of the past. *Murmuring of assent.*
Shot 648.
Medium close-up of the HEADMASTER. *He has the*
measure of the occasion.
HEADMASTER : But in point of fact, there can be few places
where tradition is examined with such a critical eye as this
College.
Shot 649.
Overhead shot of a section of the audience: STEPHANS *is*
sitting demurely next to his mother, KEATING, *still*
moody, behind him.
HEADMASTER *off* : A constant self-appraisal is going on, and
indeed, changes are happening . . .
Shot 650.
Medium long shot of another section of the audience:
BRUNNING *sitting with his parents,* MRS. KEMP *and*
MATRON *behind.*
HEADMASTER *off* : . . . so fast that even as I speak, these
words are out of date. *Laughter.*
Shot 651.
Medium long shot of the HEADMASTER: *behind him the*
MASTERS *and important guests.*
HEADMASTER : But first, I want to introduce General Denson,

who, of course, needs no introduction, either as a national hero, or as an Old Boy. General Denson.

The HEADMASTER *turns to* GENERAL DENSON *who gets up and strides briskly to the front of the stage. Everybody claps.*
Shot 652.
Medium long shot of the audience applauding: BRUNNING *again.*

GENERAL *off*: Thank you, Headmaster.
Shot 653.
Medium long shot of GENERAL DENSON *standing on the stage. The* HEADMASTER *has sat down in the centre, next to the* BISHOP. *The* GENERAL *speaks like the fine old no-nonsense war horse that he is.*

GENERAL: Your Royal Highness, my Lord Bishop, my Lords, Ladies and Gentlemen, Men of College. Now you chaps are probably thinking there's nothing much an old soldier like me can teach you. Well, you may be right. All the same I'm going to have a shot at it. *Polite amusement from the audience.* First thing—
Shot 654.
Medium shot of a group of BOYS *sitting nicely in a row, with visitors behind them.*

GENERAL *off*: You're lucky! Yes—a lot of men would give their eye-teeth to be sitting where you're sitting now. You are privileged. Now . . .
Shot 655.
Close-up of some BOYS.

GENERAL *off*: . . . for heaven's sake don't get me wrong. There is nothing the matter with privilege . . .
Shot 656.
Close-up of more BOYS *looking towards the stage.*

GENERAL *off*: . . . as long as we're ready to pay for it. It's a very sad thing, but today it is fashionable . . .
Shot 657.
Medium shot of more BOYS *looking towards the stage. (Still on page 141)*

GENERAL *off*: . . . to belittle tradition. The old order that made our nation a—a living force . . .

Shot 658.

Back to GENERAL DENSON *in medium close-up.*

GENERAL : . . . are, for the most part, scorned by modern psychiatrists, priests, pundits of all sorts. But what have they got to put in their place, hmm? Oh, politicians talk . . .

Shot 659.

High angle medium shot of a group of mothers in a variety of hats; on the other side of the aisle is a similar group of BOYS.

GENERAL *off* : . . . a lot about freedom. Well, freedom is the heritage of every Englishman, ' who speaks with the tongue that Shakespeare spoke ' . . .

Shot 660.

Close-up of a senior R.A.F. officer, with handlebar moustache, listening attentively. Behind him MATRON *and* MRS. KEMP *follow every word.*

GENERAL *off* : But, you know, we won't stay free unless we're ready to fight.

Shot 661.

Close-up of an elderly lady, with a hat like a crimson shower of petals. She looks as if there is plenty of fight in her.

GENERAL *off* : And you won't be any good as fighters unless you know something about discipline.

Shot 662.

Medium close-up of a man seated: a bourgeois paterfamilias, approving.

GENERAL *off* : The habit of obedience, how to give orders, and how to take them.

Shot 663.

Medium close-up of two women, seen in profile: two Volumnias of the Empire.

GENERAL *off* : Never mind the sneers of the cynics. *Someone starts to cough.* Let us just be true to honour . . .

Shot 664.

Long shot of GENERAL DENSON *on the stage. He looks out over the audience. As he speaks, smoke starts to seep through the floorboards at his feet, but he does not notice.* MR. KEMP *points a worried finger;* MR. STEWART *seems*

159

to shake.

GENERAL : . . . duty . . . national pride. We still *need* loyalty . . . *Several people in the audience are beginning to cough . . .* we still *need* tradition. If we look round us at the world today, what do we see? *Smoke is now visible.* We see bloodshed, confusion, decay. I know the world has changed a great deal in the past fifty years . . .

Shot 665.

High angle medium long shot of PARENTS *and* BOYS *including* MATRON *and* MRS. KEMP. *People are fidgeting, murmuring among themselves, pointing to the stage, putting handkerchiefs over their noses. The smoke is now clearly visible as it wafts across the Hall.*

GENERAL *off* : . . . But England, our England, doesn't change so easily . . .

Shot 666.

Close-up of GENERAL DENSON'S *feet. Smoke is now pouring up between the floorboards.*

GENERAL *off* : . . . And back here in College today . . .

Shot 667.

Medium shot of the BISHOP. *The* HEADMASTER *is looking worriedly at the smoke, and up at* GENERAL DENSON, *who continues to talk. The* BISHOP *looks flustered.* ROWNTREE *comes over to the* HEADMASTER. *They confer in whispers, as the smoke gets thicker in front of them. The* HEADMASTER *sends* ROWNTREE *off to investigate.*

GENERAL : . . . I feel, and it makes me jolly proud, that there is still a tradition here . . .

Shot 668.

High angle medium long shot of the audience, including FORTINBRAS *and* BARNES. *They are looking anxiously towards the smoke, and cannot decide whether or not to interrupt the proceedings. An elderly woman in a scarlet turban gets up and edges her way out, followed by her husband. She holds a handkerchief to her face.*

GENERAL *off* : . . . which has not changed, and by God, it isn't going to change.

Coughing mingles with never-say-die applause.

Shot 669.

160

Low angle medium shot of one of the MASTERS *and a* KNIGHT, *monumentally seated as smoke billows around them.*

GENERAL *off* : It's up to all of you chaps to give the world a . . .

Shot 670.
High angle shot of the audience: the smoke is winning. In twos and threes, PARENTS *rise and hurry or stumble out, escorted by their sons.*

GENERAL *off* : . . . lead. It is Britain's traditions that you have learnt here. Self-reliance . . .

Shot 671.
Medium shot of the HEADMASTER *and the* BISHOP *sitting behind the* GENERAL. *The* HEADMASTER'S *composure is rapidly deserting him: he rises and makes a nervous gesture towards* GENERAL DENSON. *But the* GENERAL, *carried away by sentiment and fervour, is still oblivious of what is happening.*

GENERAL : . . . Service and sacrifice, the tradition of . . .

Shot 672.
Medium long shot of the crowd, seen from the back as they hurry down the aisle. We see a KNIGHT *hurry with them. The smoke billows through the hall: the coughing and spluttering intensify.*

GENERAL *off* : . . . College. And it's up to all of us to reassure the world . . .

Shot 673.
Long shot from the back of the Hall: the HEADMASTER *and* GENERAL *are on the front of the stage. The crowd of* PARENTS, *with* STEPHANS *and* FORTINBRAS *among them, are now on the move, a* KNIGHT *in the middle of them. Many of them are already pushing their way out of the Hall. Chairs are knocked over as more people hurry out.* GENERAL DENSON *can still just be seen through the smoke, standing on the stage at the far end of the Hall, still speaking.*

GENERAL : . . . by our unquestioning obedience that we still hold . . . *The* GENERAL *breaks off, noticing the smoke for the first time. He raises his arms and shouts at the people hurrying*

161

out . . . My God, we're on fire! Now don't panic! Don't panic! Women first . . . Break open the windows . . .

His voice is soon drowned in the general hubbub. The rush for the door becomes panic-stricken, as everyone crushes together in the aisle. ROWNTREE *pushes his way through the shouting* BOYS *and hysterical mothers, trying to calm them and get some order into the escape. The* STAFF *begin to pour off the stage. (Still on page 141)*
Shot 674.
High angle shot from the stage. The BISHOP *hurls himself past camera and down the steps, bunching his robes in one hand, brandishing his crook in the other. The College* PORTER *struggles against the tide below, trying to reach and protect his master. The* HEADMASTER *hurries down into the crowd, followed by the* KNIGHT.
Shot 675.
Long shot from the back of the Hall. Pandemonium. Not panic (of course) but near it. People shove and push through the smoke. MACHIN, *his surplice flying, hops gleefully from chair to chair.* ROWNTREE *issues his commands impotently in the middle of the crowd: the* WHIPS *shout and gesture. Everyone is pushing for the doors.*

GENERAL *shouting above the noise* :
> ' Stand up! Stand up, for College!
> Each manly voice up-raise! '

Shot 676.
High angle shot down the corridor outside: the crowd surges forward, shouting and clattering. Camera pans left of BOYS *hopping over chairs by the wall, then tracks back in the middle of the frightened, coughing throng.* STEPHANS *and* KEATING *are barging through, regardless. The crowd of mothers, fathers,* STAFF *and* BOYS *is moving faster than the camera. It is a compulsive stampede for the open air.*
Shot 677.
High angle, very long shot of the sunlit quad outside. Across the green turf, through a grey stone archway, smoke is billowing forth. The first PARENTS *and* STAFF

to escape spill out into the open, coughing and gasping for air. Others pour out thankfully behind them. A few moments calm. Then a sudden, ear-shattering explosion. A flash of flame. A column of smoke goes up as a shell explodes on the lawn. PARENTS fall, stunned or dead. Others look up and run for cover. (Still on page 142)
Shot 678.
Low angle, violent zoom in to MICK pouring rapid Bren gun fire down into the quad from an angle in the roof. Beside him the GIRL feeds him with new magazines. MICK wears a leather flying jacket and his College trousers. The GIRL has an old camouflage jacket and ammunition belts. A Sten gun is slung from her shoulder. (Still on page 142)
Shot 679.
Overhead long shot of the gate and the quad from MICK's position. Men, women and BOYS pour out with the smoke, to be met by a hail of bullets. They look up, panic, scatter for cover against the walls. Some fall.
Shot 680.
Low angle shot of JOHNNY, astride the roof, firing a Sten gun, wearing a flying jacket and a yellow scarf. Camera pans with him as he slithers down.
Shot 681.
Medium long shot from ground level as people scatter from gunfire. (Still on page 142) BOYS and men help their mothers, crouching against walls and buttresses. Bodies are strewn on the grass.
Shot 682.
Close-up of JOHNNY, spraying the crowd with his Sten.
Shot 683.
Three MASTERS sprint over a corner of the quad, gowns and hoods flapping. A shell explodes at their heels.
Shot 684.
Medium shot of BOBBY PHILLIPS, in khaki sweater, handing a mortar shell up to WALLACE, who is standing by the mortar barrel.
Shot 685.
Reverse medium shot : WALLACE, in peaked forage cap,

163

*white sweater, and leather jerkin, slips the shell into the
barrel of the mortar.*
Shot 686.
Close-up of PHILLIPS: *he shields his ears.*
Shot 687.
Close-up of the mortar: the shell fires.
Shot 688.
*High angle shot of the quad path. Figures running.
Another explosion.*
Shot 689.
Medium close-up: WALLACE *moves along the parapet,
towards camera, firing bursts from his Sten.* PHILLIPS
crouches in foreground.
Shot 690.
*Long shot of the quad: more people seeking cover
against the crowded buttresses. One of the* KNIGHTS *lopes
along in his heavy armour, his red cloak flapping, camera
panning with him.*
Shot 691.
Low angle medium shot of the GIRL *firing her Sten over
the battlements. (Still on page 142)* MICK *is on the roof
behind, firing. Zoom in to a close-up of the* GIRL, *firing
savagely.*
Shot 692.
High angle shot of the HEADMASTER *running desperately
along the wall, camera panning with him. Bullets ricochet
off the path at his feet. Camera holds, then pans with
him as he checks and makes for a buttress.*
Shot 693.
Low angle medium shot of JOHNNY, *gone berserk with
his Sten.*
Shot 694.
Overhead shot of MASTERS *and* BOYS *crouched against
a buttress. One* BOY *panics and tries to run out : the*
CHAPLAIN *drags him back into safety. A mother crawls
hysterically round the buttress.*
Shot 695.
Low angle shot: MICK *strides to a new position on the
roof, firing from the hip as he goes. Camera pans with*

164

*him, holding as he reaches a protective gable. He fires
steadily into the foreground.*
Shot 696.
Long shot of the mêlée on the ground. The BISHOP *has
now emerged from the smoke. He runs like a terrified
stag, the camera panning as he reverses direction and
scoots along the wall, crook wildly waving, to the*
GENERAL'S *car.*
VOICE *off* : Keep down. Back against the wall.
Shot 697.
Medium shot of WALLACE *blazing away. He steadies
himself with a foot on the parapet.*
Shot 698.
High angle medium long shot: GENERAL DENSON *runs
past cowering* PARENTS *to his staff car. Camera pans
with him and zooms into medium shot as one of the
M.P.'s hands him a rifle.*
Shot 699.
Low angle shot of JOHNNY, *knee up on a parapet: a
savage burst of fire. (Still on page 142)*
Shot 700.
*The quad: white figures scattering; a mother in a white
dress waddles hysterically across the grass.*
Shot 701.
High angle shot of GENERAL DENSON : *he fires once—
then turns, barking out orders to all around.*
GENERAL : Ammunition quick! Break open the Armoury!
Rapping impatiently on the bonnet of his car. Every man a
rifle. Now keep low! Keep low! Rabbit-crawl! *He ducks
down as a bullet ricochets off the bonnet of the car.*
Shot 702.
Low angle shot of MICK *firing his Bren ferociously
through the battlements.*
Shot 703.
A KNIGHT *ventures forward from a buttress: a ricochet
sends him back. (Still on page 142)*
Shot 704.
*High angle medium shot of one of the M.P.'s firing up.
Camera pans to the other M.P., also firing. They are*

165

crouched behind their motorcycles. BOYS, *women and a* KNIGHT *rabbit-crawl across the background.*
Shot 705.
Medium shot: a crowd of PARENTS *besiege the Armoury. Agressive cries and greedy arms outstretched. The* CHAPLAIN *hands out rifles:* PARENTS *seize them.*
Shot 706.
GENERAL *directs the counter-attack from behind his car.*
GENERAL: Infiltrate their flank. Get a Bren gun on their flank! Come on! Jump to it!
Shot 707.
High angle shot as feet charge forward over the grass: in the background an aged PARENT *lies firing among* BOYS. *A spatter of bullets rips across the turf. A running army officer twists and falls.*
Shot 708.
Medium shot of FORTINBRAS: *he kneels in front of the* GENERAL'S *car, firing up with a Sten.* PARENTS *creep and huddle behind him. A father fires a rifle at his side.*
Shot 709.
Close-up of a woman. She is lying on the ground, covering her head with her hands. Her eyes twitch as the world explodes around her.
Shot 710.
Medium shot: a large, fur-coated lady firing a Sten gun. Her face is grim. BOYS *and other women crouch down.*
WOMAN *between bursts*: Bastards! Bastards! Bastards!
Shot 711.
Medium close-up of BARNES *kneeling on the grass, firing a Sten. The* HEADMASTER *hurries up behind him.*
Shot 712.
Long shot of the quad: firing; people running in the background. The HEADMASTER *strides forward towards camera, every inch a leader.*
HEADMASTER *pleading, calling up and to the people round him*: Stop firing! Cease fire! Cease firing! *The firing dies down. He pleads to the fighters on the rooftop, his arms outstretched.* Boys, boys, boys! I understand you . . . listen to reason and trust me! Trust me!

166

Shot 713.

MICK *and the* GIRL *on the roof:* MICK *holds his Bren gun, relaxed. He glances round as the* GIRL *draws her pistol from her belt and aims it deliberately down. Zoom into close-up. The pistol fires. (Still on page 143)*

Shot 714.

Close-up of the HEADMASTER. *Blood trickles down from the hole in the middle of his forehead. (Still on page 143) He sinks down out of frame, his movement slowed . . . Nobody moves. The only sound is the wind whistling.*

Shot 715.

*High angle long shot as a mortar shell explodes in the middle of the quad. With the crash, the organ bursts in heavily with the College song. Firing; rifles and grenades. In two waves, from right and left, the attack comes in —*PARENTS, MASTERS, BOYS. *A machine gun is positioned and opens fire.* MATRON *lobs grenades.*

Shot 716.

Close-up of the barrel of MICK'S *Bren gun; it is firing continuously; flame and smoke. It disappears out of frame as* MICK *slides down the roof and into close-up, still firing.*

Shot 717.

High angle long shot of the quad: smoke fills the air as the attackers unite in their barrage of fire. The music is drowned out. The BISHOP *stands crook in hand, as rifles, machine guns, grenades explode from all sides. (Still on page 144)*

Shot 718.

Close-up of MICK *frantically blazing away with his Sten gun—a continuous torrent of bullets. Camera holds on him: his face desperate, unyielding. (Still on page 144)*

Shot 719.

Cut to black. Silence.

Fade in to superimposed title (scarlet).

TITLE : **if. . . .**

Fade out.[1]

———————

[1] End of reel six.